OVERCOMING ADVERSITY

Pijhon Valcourt

Copyright ©2016
OVERCOMING ADVERSITY
by
Pijhon Valcourt

All rights reserved. No part of this book may be reproduced in any form without permission in writing from the author or publisher.

ISBN # 978-1-943847-72-3

Library of Congress Cataloging
in -Publication Data

Valcourt, Pijhon

First Printing 2016
Printed in the U.S.A.

This book is dedicated to Alex, Nay Nay, Scooby, Kai, and Papo. Just know that you can overcome any adversity that life brings your way. I love you all.

CONTENTS

ACKNOWLEDGMENTS		vii
1	THE DIVORCE	1
2	THE MOLESTED	13
3	THE MOLESTED II	23
4	THE HEARTBREAK	31
5	THE MOLESTED III	41
6	THE FELON	49
7	THE RELIGION	59
8	THE RECRUIT	69
9	THE DRUG DEALER	79
10	THE ABUSED	89
11	THE LONELY ONE	99
12	THE CAT EATER	109
13	THE END	119

ACKNOWLEDGEMENTS

I would like to take the time out to thank everyone who has played a part in me accomplishing my dreams and goals. Your guidance, knowledge, and expertise have helped me become the person that I am today. This has been a long journey but it has been well worth the wait. Thank you.

Introduction

What is adversity? It can be best described as a state of hardship or affliction. All of us at some point or another in our lives have dealt with some form of adversity. I believe that when one goes through adversity during adolescence, it better prepares them for it as an adult. This is not always the case but I have seen many examples of it, myself being one. Those that have not experienced it through adolescence many times do not have the coping mechanisms to handle it as an adult. I am not talking about minor hardships. I am talking about being sexually assaulted, dealing with infidelity, divorce, foreclosure, etc. Those are adversities that can drive someone to the breaking point.

The purpose of this book is to share with you experiences of adversity within my life and of those that I have had the pleasure of coming into contact with. Some of those experiences were handled well, while others could have benefited from an alternative approach. Either way, something can be taken away from each experience. I just want you to know if you are going through a hardship right now, it will be alright. You have the ultimate control over your life. If you choose to let adversity dictate your happiness, then it shall. If you are reading this book, then something has guided you to it for a reason. I would like to think that reason is for you to use this book as a tool to help strengthen you and help overcome whatever hardship that has affected you or someone you may know.

In this book you will read stories of individuals who have experienced adversities but did not let it define them. There are also stories of some who have a hard time dealing with those hardships. There will also be tips throughout the book on how to cope with the adversities that come in life. To respect the privacy of those individuals who wished to remain anonymous, names and identifying details have been changed. In this book there are things that will make you laugh and some things that may make you cry. Ultimately there will be something in here that you can relate to and use in your time of need, should it come. Enjoy the book and share it with someone who you feel may need it.

WHAT WE CAN CONTROL IS OUR OWN BEHAVIOR.

Chapter 1

The Divorce

*"Action may not always bring happiness,
but there is no happiness without action."*
~William James

I was officially married for approximately ten years. I can honestly say that there were about five good years and five bad ones. She was the girl of my dreams. We met in middle school and I loved her at first sight. The first year of knowing her I never said a word to her. We had all the same classes but never sat by each other. I would pray all year that we got assigned a project together or something so I could have an excuse to speak to her. My prayers were never answered that year. The next year God did his thing though and put us sitting right next to each other. I guess God works on his schedule and not mine.

We instantly hit it off. She was beautiful, smart, and funny. We would play pranks on each other in class, but most of the times I would get caught by the teacher and get in trouble. I did not mind it though. I was a fool for beautiful girls at that age, now I am a fool for beautiful women. Some things never change. I was really digging her though. Towards the end of middle school, I wrote her a letter, or rather a note letting her know that I really liked her. I almost gave it to her, but chickened out and threw it away. I was too shy at that age to let her know my true feelings, so of course I got sent straight to the friend zone. We became the best of friends. She would open up and tell me any and everything. I would naturally do the same with her as well.

The friendship carried on to high school. Many of my friends questioned why I was not dating her. I would always tell them that she was just my friend and that I did not see her like that. Obviously that was a big fat lie, but I could not tell them that I was too scared to let her know my true feelings and that I was a prisoner in the friend zone. After I told them that we were just friends, they would hit on her. This friendship was torture at times.

Being that we were best friends, she would tell me about the boyfriends she had and issues that came up in their relationship. I would give her my advice on the issues she had. I would tell her about my girlfriends and issues as well so she could give me her input. No matter who I was dating though, I knew she would be my wife one day. I had prayed and wished about it many times. She was my soul mate and we were destined to be together.

We eventually graduated high school and I went to the military. She ended up staying at home in order to go to college. We constantly stayed in touch with each other while I was away. I wrote her letters and sent her postcards from the various countries that I visited. I remember the night before I left for basic training; we stayed outside talking until about four in the morning. I told her whatever she does; do not get pregnant while I was away. She did not listen and would eventually have a child while I was in the service. When she told me that news, I cannot even lie, I was a little disappointed. I wanted her to have my kids. Little did I know, she would eventually give me three beautiful children. Technically it would be four kids because I took her daughter as my own. From the first day I met that little girl a bond was formed between us that would never be broken.

While I was in the last year of my contract with the military, I invited her to come up and visit me on the base. At that time I had just gotten off of a six month deployment overseas. While I was on that deployment, I got news that a woman I was dating had sex with one of my friends. That kind of broke my heart, so when I got back to base I had vowed to be a player for life. There would be no relationship for me. I did not want anything serious and I let all the women know what time it was. I was having fun being a player. Once again, a higher power had a different plan in store for me.

When she arrived to the base, one thing led to another and we crossed that friendship line. I was not in the friend zone anymore. It was a great and magically night. All the years of fantasizing of what it would be like with my dream girl finally came true. She stayed the whole weekend with me and everything felt right. She did not want to leave. She actually cried when she left. When she got back home we had a conversation on what we were going to do next. I can honestly say that I thought we were just going to just remain friends. I still had a year left in my contract and I did not want to get into anything serious. She did not feel the same way.

An ultimatum was kind of given to me. We would either be together or we could not be friends anymore. I did not want to lose my best friend so I proposed to her. I would use that ultimatum as a weapon to throw in her face during our marriage. The truth is, she was not to blame. It was me for not being honest. I was not ready to get married at that time. I should have been man enough to tell her that. We should have dated for a little while first. We knew each other as best friends, but not as lovers. That would be detrimental in our marriage.

Soon after that proposal we decided to get married. She went back home and broke the news to all the guys she was dealing with and I did the same to the females in my life. My friends could not believe it. They were use to me saying how I was a player and that no one would tie me down. The one woman who had my heart called upon it, and I answered. This player was off the market.

We decided that there would be no big church wedding. We did not want a crowd of people at our wedding. We did it the "courthouse" way. It would be a day that I would never forget. I was in another state so I drove twelve hours to make it to the courthouse. On the way to the courthouse, I was about one hour away when I got a flat tire. I did not have a spare so I was stuck on the expressway on my wedding day, an hour away from my bride to be. I had to walk about three miles to get a new tire. As I walked along the expressway, I wondered if this was a sign to not go through with getting married. I dismissed the thought and proceeded to change the tire and resume with my plans to pick up my bride.

As soon as I arrived to pick up my soon to be wife, the car started smoking about ten minutes away from the courthouse. I did not know what it was; my car had never done anything like that before. So I looked under the hood, not knowing what I was doing. I did a little moving of some hoses and messing around with some wires. Eventually the car stopped smoking and we were on our way. I thought again about that being a sign not to go through with the wedding, but I dismissed that as well.

We finally got to the courthouse and there were no more issues until that night. We ended up getting a hotel room so we could consummate our marriage. Unfortunately while I was in the room getting busy, someone was getting busy breaking into my car. They stole my radio and speakers. They also stole her purse out of the car. As I think back on that day, I wonder if all the things that happened to me that day were signs that I should not have gotten married. Nonetheless, married I was.

When the marriage was good, it consisted of family vacations, great communication, and financial prosperity. When it was bad, it consisted of infidelity, constant arguing, and resentment. I cannot blame all the issues we had all on her. I believe we both played an equal role in the destruction of the marriage. We slowly began to fall out of love with each other. When I would come home from work I would be in the living room watching television, while she was in the bedroom watching television.

We began to do many things separate instead of as a married couple. The last year of the marriage I slept on the couch. I started sleeping on the couch when my youngest son was born in order to give her room in the bed with him. I slept kind of wild in the bed and I did not want to crush him. Eventually he got older and when it was time to come back in the bed to sleep with her, I did not want to. I enjoyed sleeping alone on the couch. This is a very bad sign in a marriage. If the two of you are not bonding physically and mentally, disaster is sure to follow. If you and your spouse are constantly doing things separately, do whatever you have to do to change that.

It came to a point where we were just arguing all the time. Resentment had set in on both sides and the seeds of the divorce were firmly planted. I was contemplating divorce for a while at this point, but every time I would think about the kids I would remove the thought from my head. I knew she wanted out as well but she would never say it. I would have to be the one to make the move. This was a tough time in my life. I was afraid of losing my house, my kids, and finances. A divorce is written documentation that your marriage has failed. I did not want to be a failure but I wanted happiness as well.

We were just living what I called the lie. We both were not happy but we had to keep the lie going for the kids. I wonder how many of you out there are living or have lived the lie. We had to keep the lie going on for our family and friends as well. Many people in this world live those lies for various reasons. I could not do it anymore. I was so unhappy that I was willing to lose all my finances and my house just for my happiness. It was at that point where I chose my happiness above all did things start to change. Before those changes came, I had to sit my kids down and break the news of the divorce to them. Now let me tell you something about that. To tell them that was one of the hardest things that I had to ever do in my life. I can still see their faces when the words came out of my mouth. Tears came down their eyes and I fought so hard to keep my tears in. It was a very sad and dark time for me and my family. I could not see the light through all that darkness but the light would eventually come.

    I decided that no matter what, I would make this divorce as painless as possible for my kids. Whatever my ex-wife wanted, she could have. My pride was out the window. I found that when we both made it about the kids, it worked. On the day of the divorce we rode together in the car. We were in and out of the courtroom in about ten minutes. The judge made a comment that our divorce was one of the quickest that he ever had. We were both unhappy and we decided to do something about it. By no means am I advocating divorce for someone who is going through issues in their marriage. Everyone has to make whatever decision that they feel is right for them. My ex-wife and I were in a cycle of happiness, destruction, resentment, and unhappiness. This went on for ten years.

    I realized that I could start over. One of my college professors, Kion McGhee, told me one of the most inspiring stories that I will always remember. He was at home sleep in the bed with his wife one morning when his phone started to ring. It was real early in the morning so he did not answer. The person kept calling so his wife decided to answer it. A female was on the line and she asked to speak to him. I'm guessing his wife was used to him receiving calls from various people, women included. He is also an attorney. Anyway, his wife told the woman that he was asleep.

Professor McGhee felt that something was strange about the call so he decided to call the woman back. When he did, it turned out that she was a student of his. She was crying hysterically. She told him that she had a gun and that she was going to shoot herself. Professor McGhee told her that he was in his bed with his wife and that she could go ahead and shoot herself. I am guessing that he felt this would deter her because who would actually tell someone with a gun to shoot themselves.

After a short pause, he heard a loud gunshot. The professor was astonished. He thought that this student had called him for help and he told her to shoot herself. Luckily she had just shot in the air, but at this point he really knew she had a gun. She stated to him again that she was really going to kill herself. Professor McGhee told her that she was not going to do it, because if she was she would have done it already. Clearly she wanted help so that is why she called him. He arranged to meet with her at a local café in about an hour.

Once at the café he sat down with her and asked her what was the problem. She told him that she had just lost her job, she was losing her house in foreclosure, and her husband had abandoned her. The professor looked at her and began to give her solutions to each one of her problems. For her losing her job, he told her to get another one. There are many people hiring and just like she got that job, she would get another one. For her losing her house in foreclosure, he told her that she has a burden lifted. She does not have to worry about paying a mortgage. There are many people renting houses and apartments so let the bank have the house. And finally, to the issue of her husband abandoning her, he told her to find another husband. There are many men on this earth besides her husband that would be more than willing to date or marry her.

When it all boiled down, Professor McGhee told her that those were not her main concerns. The real issue she had was what people would think of her. It was the perception of herself to others that was really bothering her. He told her that people are going through the same issues as her so she had nothing to be ashamed of. Professor McGhee told her that you can hit the reset button as many times in life as you want. Many people fear of how other people will see them when they are going through adversities. I have a little secret for you all, other people have adversities of their own, so do not think that it is unique to you.

After hitting my own reset button, amazing things started to happen. I did not lose my house, I did not lose all my finances, and I could spend time with my kids anytime I wanted to. All the credit cannot be taken by me on this. Without a collaborative effort by my ex-wife, things could have turned out differently. Some of you may have exes that are impossible to deal with. My advice to you would be to lead by example. We cannot control another person's behavior. If someone wants to be difficult, they will be difficult. What we can control is our own behavior. The sooner that concept resonates, the easier things will be.

The adversity of divorce is a difficult situation to deal with. My ex-wife and I bump heads every now and then but we always keep in perspective that we are raising kids. With that perspective in mind, we can usually resolve whatever issue that comes up. If you happen to be going through the adversity of divorce, just remember that you will get through it. You may not see the light, neither did I. Trust me when I tell you that the light is there and it is waiting to shine on you.

WHAT WAS DONE TO YOU DOES NOT DEFINE WHO YOU ARE.

Chapter 2

The Molested

"It is not what they take from you that counts. It's what you do with what you have left."
~Hubert Humphrey

I happen to have a lot of female friends. Many have disclosed personal secrets that they have not shared with others. Women that I have dated also have shared intimate secrets as well. Some of those secrets have to do with sexual molestations. This is an issue that is plaguing many families. If you have been a victim of sexual molestation, ask yourself how many other people do you know that have also been a victim. If you are not a victim, ask yourself how many victims do you know. The perpetrators in many of these cases are family members or close family friends. Most of these women have never reported the incidents. Some still deal with these people to this day. Parents should especially be cautious with young children with regards to this issue. These predators are closer than you think to your children.

One woman who shared her story with me was Patricia. Now Patricia is as "hood" as they come. I do not say that to be insulting by any means. I grew up in the hood, so this term is used endearingly. She is a feisty one who will not take crap from anyone. Her slim build, small stature, and many tattoos would lead one to believe that she was an exotic dancer, but she was far from that. When I first met her, I was drawn to her instantly. Something in my soul commanded me to go and approach her, so of course I listened to my soul and made my introduction. After speaking to her for about five minutes, she began to cry. I was trying to get her number, but it was obvious that she was in so much pain. She told me about how her ex-boyfriend used to beat her; burn her with cigarettes, among many other heinous acts. I was a stranger and she felt so comfortable to reveal these personal things to me. Many people hide their issues until after a couple of dates, but not Patricia, she was putting it out there upfront. I do not know if this was to deter me from talking to her or she was just hurting so bad that she could not hide it. She seemed broken to me and I wanted to "fix" her. I guess it is that hero complex in me or maybe the healer in me that wants to soothe a person's pain. Patricia was hurting. This would be a very tall order for me.

We would go out on a couple of dates and it was apparent that we did not have that much in common, but the conversations were not bad. We maintained a friendship in which we would go out from time to time. She would reveal even more pain and torture that she endured during many of her relationships. Being newly single, I was just looking for a sexual connection with her, but this was not going to be that type of friendship. There was a bigger plan and purpose at hand that I did not even know about.

One night Patricia came to my house to hang out. We sat on the couch and began to talk. She just began opening up about her life and how rough she had it. This friendship seemed more like a doctor / patient relationship. She talked and cried for about two hours straight. I had never met someone carrying so much pain inside of them. This woman seemed like she was suffering from PTSD (Post Traumatic Stress Disorder). I am not a doctor to diagnose anything, but something about her just screamed PTSD to me. She was like a war veteran returning from a war zone. She actually told me that she wished that she was still with one of her exes. Even though he used to beat her, she felt that he actually loved her. Something in her mistook that physical abuse for love. For those who have never experienced domestic violence, it is hard to comprehend, but nonetheless it is their reality. I just held her as she cried and talked. So where did all this pain originate from with her? When she told me her story, it all made sense.

    As far back as she could remember she was a happy loving child. She was carefree with no worries at all. In the early years of her life it was just Patricia's mother and her siblings. Patricia was around the age of four when her mother met Dennis. She did not really know her father at that age but Dennis was going to be that father figure to her, so she thought. She could remember being so excited to finally have a dad in the house.

    Patricia's mother was a very beautiful woman. All the guys in the neighborhood wanted a piece of her; unfortunately Dennis was the lucky guy who got her. Patricia did not really see anything wrong with Dennis at first; monsters usually wear masks in order to blend in with the rest of us. He would check on her when she took baths. If he had to run an errand, he would make sure that she rode with him in the car. Even when she would play outside with her friends, he would call her inside just to sit next to him. Dennis would make comments on how big her butt was and would constantly want her to dance in front of family and friends. This all seemed innocent at the time. Unfortunately, Patricia was too young to know that this bastard was setting things up so he could rob her of her innocence.

One of the earliest instances of him violating her that she could remember occurred one night when everyone was sleep in the house. Patricia was lying in the bed with her siblings when she awoke to Dennis picking her up out of the bed and carrying her. Where was he taking her in the middle of the night? Where was her mother? Those questions were soon made apparent as they reached their destination, the hallway closet. I do not think she could ever clearly explain how confused, scared, and hurt she was at what happened next. This coward pulled down her panties and began rubbing her vaginal and anal area. He used Vaseline to lubricate her anus. He then proceeded to anally penetrate her with his penis. Patricia knew nothing of sex at that age. At five years old she was subjected to this kind of brutality. Why had she been chosen to suffer like that? As a young child you want to feel protected. This act that Dennis committed was the death of her childhood. When Dennis was done violating her he put back on her panties and carried her back to her bed. All the while Patricia's mother slept in the other room oblivious to what was happening to her child.

From the ages of five to eleven Patricia was continually molested and raped by this man. He would continually take her from her bed at night and into the hallway closet. Dennis became so bold that when he had his friends over to play video games, he would sit Patricia in his lap. While in his lap, he would stick his hand in her underwear and fondle her. To this day she does not know if his friends knew what was going on. If they did know what was going on, how could they allow this to happen to her? This just makes you wonder how you never really know what is going on with people. I would feel awful knowing that I was visiting a friend and he was molesting his child right under my nose. It is sad to say but this thing happens every day. As you read this, some child is being subjected to this type of torture.

This cycle of hell for Patricia included Dennis constantly watching her bathe, smelling her dirty panties that were in the hamper, and continually dragging her out of the bed in the middle of the night and into the closet. Patricia used to bury herself under her siblings at night, hoping that Dennis could not find her in the bed, but to no avail he always did. Other kids were hiding from imaginary monsters under their beds; unfortunately Patricia was hiding from the real thing in her room. Now I do not really cry much, but listening to Patricia telling me this story almost brought tears to my eyes. I had to be strong for her and listen. After a while Patricia pretty much got used to being violated, or rather numb to it. I guess that was her coping mechanism for dealing with it.

One night as Patricia and Dennis were in the closet, her mother came in and turned on the lights. She asked what was going on and why was Patricia out the bed and in the closet. Dennis must have heard her coming because he made sure her panties were back on. He told her mother that she was having nightmares and that he was trying to calm her down. There was no way in hell that her mother believed that I thought. To top it off, he was such in a rush to put on her panties that he put them on backwards. An observation that her mother quickly observed. Patricia's mother questioned that as well. Patricia was sent to her room while her mother and Dennis remained in the hallway.

They argued for a long time about why Patricia was in the closet with him and why her panties were on backwards. Dennis continually denied doing anything. Her mother eventually came to Patricia's room and interrogated her on whether Dennis touched her or did anything inappropriate. Her mother swore that she would kill him if he did. Patricia knew this and did not want her mother to go to jail for killing that man, so she lied. This is a common reason given by people who were molested for not telling. They fear that their parents would retaliate and go to jail, so they remain silent. They do not want to lose their parents. How many of you out there tell your kids that you would kill or seriously hurt anyone who hurts them? You may not really mean it, but your kids do not really know that.

Patricia kept telling her mother that Dennis never touched her. Her mother grilled and grilled but Patricia held firm to her lie. To this day, she regrets not telling her mother the truth. Soon after that incident, Patricia's mother would eventually leave Dennis; unfortunately it was after he stabbed her in the face one day during a violent argument. She survived the attack and moved on with her life. Patricia's mother is no longer living, she died of cancer a few years back. On her death bed Patricia came real close to telling her mother about what Dennis did to her when she was young, but she did not have the courage to do it. A decision she regrets to this day.

    What happened to Patricia has had a major effect on her life. She has never gotten counseling for it, as with many victims like her who have never reported what happened to them. Patricia has been in one abusive relationship after another. This has made it real hard for her to be intimate with her boyfriends. She feels as if she could have been further in life if this situation had not occurred.

    After opening up and telling her story, Patricia has begun to deal with all the pain that she has inside of her. She refuses to be a victim to that situation anymore. She has written a letter to Dennis about everything that he did to her and how it has affected her life. Although she has not mailed it to him, just writing the letter brought her some sense of peace. One day she will muster up the courage to look Dennis up and mail him the letter.

    Currently Patricia is going to school for cosmetology. She loves doing hair and does it well. As I have told Patricia numerous times, that situation that she was subjected to by Dennis does not have to define her. This adversity of molestation is a constant battle for Patricia but she has made some improvements with picking better guys to date. If you have been unfortunate enough to have had some type of sexual molestation occur, I say it to you as well, that what was done to you does not define who you are.

YOU CAN OVERCOME ANYTHING, JUST HAVE FAITH AND BELIEVE THAT YOU CAN.

Chapter 3

The Molested II

"You never know how strong you are until being strong is the only choice you have."
~Unknown

Heather is a rare breed of woman. She and I have been friends for a long time now. If she is going through things she can call me and vice versa. She is happily married with two kids, a boy and a girl. She is very family oriented. She grew up in a loving household with her mother and her father. Both parents showered her with love. Where we came from, that was a rare thing to have both parents in the household, much less love being a part of that equation.

Heather comes from a large family. Growing up, besides her two little sisters she had loads of cousins. There were always relatives in the house either visiting or staying with them for an extended amount of time. Her family dynamic kind of reminded me of mines, at least when it came to a lot of people visiting. My mother had a big heart so she would allow friends and family members who were down on their luck to come and live with us. In a household of six brothers and sisters, it was always a full house.

Now Heather felt comfortable enough with me to disclose things she had not shared with anyone, not even her husband. When she found out that I was writing this book on adversities, she had no problem with me interviewing her. She wanted to tell her story since she has been living with this secret for a long time now. Although we try to bury our secrets, they linger on waiting for the right or wrong time to appear again.

If I could use one word to describe Heather, it would be fighter. She reminded me of my mother in that way. No matter what obstacle was thrown at Heather, she would grind hard and get through it. I am sure it had something to do with what happened to her when she was younger. She does not like to feel vulnerable, so for her to disclose this secret to me was very hard for her. She knew it was time to tell her story. This secret has caused her so much pain in her life. This experience has caused an unnatural distrust of people to her. No matter whom you are or how close you get to her, she feels that the monster will eventually come out of you, as it did with her violator.

For Heather, it began when she was ten years old. She would have this habit of waiting until it was real late to watch TV. There were only two TVs in the house, one in the living room and the other in a bedroom. With so many people in the house, Heather could not watch TV during the day because in the hierarchy of the household, she was not at the top. She had to wait until everyone was sleep and sneak into the living room to watch her shows.

One night as she sat on the couch watching TV, her favorite cousin Frank came in and sat on the couch next to her. Being from a loving family, Heather would always kiss Frank on the cheek and hug him when she saw him. This was a common practice in her culture. Frank would always take her to the store to get candy and toys. She was very comfortable with him. Frank was about thirty at the time and had several kids of his own.

As Frank sat next to Heather, she laid on his lap. This was a common thing in their house, but what Frank did next was not common at all. Frank began to open her legs and rub on her inner thighs. Naturally Heather was very confused. She was wondering why was he rubbing the inside of her thighs. Frank then proceeded to pull her underwear to the side and penetrate her vagina with the tip of one of his fingers. This lasted for about five minutes.

She was never taught about sex or inappropriate touching at that age so she did not think anything was wrong with what he was doing. Heather was just very confused. What ten year old child would not be confused if someone in their family was doing this to them and they were never taught about inappropriate touching? Many times as parents, we try to shield our kids away from the topic of sex until we feel that they are at the appropriate age. This could be a costly error. At the minimum, inappropriate touching should be discussed as early as possible. Inappropriate touching by anyone, family members included, should be emphasized as unacceptable. Even if your child is under your supervision all the time, it only takes five minutes for someone to violate them.

It was not until Frank told her to keep what he had done a secret that she knew that something was wrong with what he did to her. She had sat on his lap and hugged him numerous of times and he never said to keep those a secret, so why this? Heather did not know what to do. Nothing like this had ever happened to her. She had never kept any secrets from her parents. But this was Frank, he was her cousin and an adult. Heather was taught to respect adults so she did not want to violate his trust.

Heather decided to keep what Frank had done a secret, thinking it was just a one-time thing. Several months would pass by without anything else happening. Heather continued staying up late to watch T.V. Then one night, just like the first night, as she was up watching T.V. Frank came in and sat next to her. Heather felt very uncomfortable this time. All she could think about is what Frank had done the last time he sat next to her. She felt as if she invited the first situation by laying on him, so this time she made up in her mind that she would not lay on him. Heather thought that by not laying on him, it would send him a clear message that she did not want to be touched. Sadly Frank did not get the message, nor did he care.

This time Frank proceeded to start as he did the last time by rubbing her inner thighs. Instead of using the tip of his finger to penetrate her like last time, he penetrated her vagina with his whole finger. This hurt Heather so bad that she gripped his wrist with both of her hands, giving him a hard stare but not saying a word. Frank told her that he was teaching her how to become a woman. Heather thought to herself that she really did want to become a woman. She truly believed that this was a rite of passage in becoming a woman. So Heather just sat there as he did what he did. It seemed like an eternity for it to be over, but eventually it was done.

The abuse would continue a few more times, with Frank using multiple fingers to penetrate Heather. She eventually stopped staying up late to watch T.V. Frank knew that Heather was smart and since she stopped staying up late to watch television, he feared that she may tell her parents what he had done to her. Frank took Heather and another male cousin that she had around her same age and took them to a friend's house. While at the house, Frank told the other cousin that he must have sex with Heather. Neither one of them knew anything about sex. Frank had the two of them touch each other until he was satisfied. He then took both of them home.

Soon after that incident, Frank was still in fear that Heather would tell her parents what he did to her. He decided to tell her parents that he thought that another cousin was touching her. He put the blame on the young cousin that he forced to touch Heather. After hearing what Frank had disclosed to them, they immediately took Heather into the room. Both of her parents asked if anyone was touching her inappropriately. That was the moment where Heather could have told them about all the horrible things that Frank had done to her. Unfortunately, all Heather could think about was that machete that her father kept above the door. She knew that her father would chop Frank to pieces if she told him the truth. Heather denied being touched; she did not want her father to go to jail.

I would like to take the time out at this point to tell parents that even though you may ask your child if someone has hurt them, they may lie. Just like Patricia, Heather was afraid to tell the truth because of the fear of her parents going to jail because of retaliation. Many times in life, where there is smoke there is fire! At least some sort of further investigation of the situation should occur. Remember, kids may lie out of fear and say that nothing is wrong even though someone is hurting them. You have to really observe the behavior of your child. If there is a change in their behavior, that is a red flag.

Frank was eventually kicked out of the house but Heather would still see him at family functions. Frank would spread rumors about her that she was promiscuous. He would make it a mission to tell her that she would be nothing in life. This hurt Heather so much as a child to have been violated by Frank and to also be told that she would be nothing. Frank is still alive today, so is the hatred that she has for him. If she could tell him one thing, it would be thank you. She believes that her experience made her the strong woman that she is today. Even though she has a hard time trusting people and has some intimacy issues with her husband, she is still a fighter. Frank may have taken advantage of her physically, but he never got to take advantage of her mentally. To Frank, Heather would like to leave you with this, "Thank you, but kiss my ass you fucking bitch!"

In both the cases of Patricia and Heather, there are lessons and tips that can be taken from their adversities. For parents, you must really take the time out and evaluate who you bring around your kids. If you notice that your child is uncomfortable around someone, question why that is the case. Do not force them to be in that person's company. I would also recommend that you not allow small children to sit in the lap of too many people, especially men. I understand that everyone is not a sexual predator but nonetheless it is something to be aware of.

According to notwithmychild.org, 1 in 3 girls and 1 in 6 boys are sexually abused before their 18th birthday. The average age of a child being molested is 9 years old. Unfortunately if your child is molested, there is a 95% chance it was done by someone you know, not a stranger. With statistics like this education is the key to combating this epidemic.

For those of you who have gone through this adversity, I would like you to know that it was not your fault. Do not take the blame for something that someone did to you. If you have not sought out counseling, it may be a good idea to seek it. Talking to a trusted friend will also help. Many individuals suppress the incident so deciding to get treatment will require reliving the nightmare. In the end, you will empower yourself by addressing this issue that has most certainly affected your life.

YOU CANNOT SCREW, DRINK, EAT, OR SLEEP YOUR WAY FROM THE PAIN.

Chapter 4
The Heartbreak

"Waiting for someone else to make you happy is the best way to be sad."
~Unknown

Before I met my ex-wife, I met the girl who would change my life forever. It was my eighth grade year and I never had a girlfriend. I was a very shy kid. My confidence was low, as well as my self-esteem. I guess it was because I came from a poor family. I was not very well dressed according to middle school standards. If anyone knows anything about middle school, it can be a very cruel place. Those were the times where any insecurity you had would be fortified and be a life long struggle, unless of course you did something about it.

Even though my family did not have much money, my mom taught us strong values. One of the biggest things that she preached was education. She would always say that even though we did not have much, we did have education and that was free. Following her wisdom I was basically a straight A student. I had perfect attendance and my conduct was outstanding.

All those things meant nothing when it came to getting a girlfriend. So in order for me to be closer to some girls, I decided to take Home Economics that year. If you do not know what Home Economics is, then I am truly getting old. For all the young readers out there, Home Economics was where they taught you how to cook and sew. So naturally, it was full of girls. My plan paid off; when I got in that class it was only three boys in there, including me. I figured that my odds would be great at getting a girlfriend that year being in a Home Economics class full of young women. Due to me being shy, most of the girls in there would either cheat off of my homework or ask me for money. I was a teenage boy with no game, so of course I gave them my homework answers and my money. Something in me back then thought that if I gave a girl whatever she asked for then she would like me. How little I knew as a young boy.

    This went on for a few months until it finally happened. One of the girls was actually showing a real interest in me. She did not just want my homework answers or my money, she actually wanted to get to know me. I believe that it was fate that brought us together, if one believes in such a thing. Well actually, I can credit the Home Economics teacher for us meeting. One day she decided to change the seating arrangements of the class. She sat a girl right next to me. Her name was Crystal and she was beautiful. We were quickly drawn to each other.

    Crystal would laugh and talk with me in class all the time. We would cook, sew, and play together. I enjoyed our time in class together and did not want for it to end. I wanted to ask for her phone number but I was too scared to ask her. Did she really even like me like that? Would I make her uncomfortable by asking for her phone number?

Would she still want to be my friend? My teenage mind was going crazy. Crystal ended up making it easy for me and asked me for my phone number. I was so ecstatic to give it to her. This would be the first girl to call my house for me. Crystal eventually called and we would talk for hours and hours on the phone. I began to get really fond of her. Butterflies would swarm in my stomach when I was with her. This teenage boy was falling in love.

Our initial conversations started off innocent. We talked about school, family, and life in general. Eventually the conversations began to shift around kissing and sex. Crystal said that she had been with one person, who was her ex-boyfriend. He was a few years older than her. They would have sex all the time. When it came to my stories, I lied and told her that I had sex numerous of times. I had never had sex at that time. I was a virgin, with a capital V. I had never even kissed a girl before I met Crystal. We would finally have our first kiss after months and months of her giving me body language hints that she wanted me to kiss her. She just took the initiative one day and just kissed me. It was amazing. My first kiss, my first girlfriend, I was in love deep. Some may call it puppy love, but it was love nonetheless.

Crystal began to ask when we were going to have sex. Have sex, I had just learned how to kiss a girl. I knew nothing of this thing called sex. I just stalled and stalled with her. I kept making excuses that she could not handle me and that she was not ready. She bought those excuses for a while. That gave me the time to try and research this thing called sex. I had no access to the internet back then so

I had to do research the old fashion way, through books. Crystal actually gave me a book on the human body. This would prove helpful because I did not even know what the female body looked like. Unfortunately, before I got to really get into the book my mom found it and confiscated it like it was some porn magazine. Parents, if you do not take the time out to speak to your kids about sex they will find out about it anyway. It will most likely be the wrong information.

Time was running out for me. Crystal was becoming impatient about us having sex. She even gave me some condoms for my birthday so time was really up. Finally the big day came. We both skipped school and met at my house. My mother was at work so the house was empty. We went into my room and onto my bed. Crystal laid down on the bed and I got on top of her. We kissed for about five minutes, as my mind raced on what to do next. She took off her clothes and I did the same. I went back to kissing her because that was all that I knew how to do. Crystal eventually got tired of this and put my penis inside of her. I could not believe that this was happening. I was having sex, at least my version of it. I just laid on top of her the whole time with my penis in her not moving just kissing her. After about ten minutes she asked did I ejaculate. I told her that I did indeed ejaculate. I saw some white stuff on my penis and figured that was what she was talking about. The first time was not what I expected it to be. It kind of hurt to tell you the truth.

We would skip school two more times and have this sad version of sex without me ever ejaculating or even moving during the act. I guess Crystal finally got tired of me not moving while on top of her, so she kind of started guiding my body in an up and down motion. That was actually feeling good so I continued with that up and down motion. Then all of a sudden I got this funny feeling, something was happening. I do not think I could ever truly describe that feeling, but every man knows what I am talking about. There was something draining out of my body and it felt great. When she asked if I ejaculated, I told her yes. This was the real deal. I was hooked.

We would continue to skip school and have unprotected sex. My grades began to suffer. I got my first F that year, actually I got more than one F. I did not even care. I was in love and having sex. I wanted Crystal to be mines forever. She was showing me love and affection. She would call me handsome and smart. My mother would not even compliment me like that. Even though I knew my mother loved me, Crystal was actually telling me and showing me. For all the kids that called me ugly, it did not matter because Crystal thought I was handsome. She was my world.

After a while things started to get a little rocky between Crystal and me. She began to get jealous of the female friends I had; my ex-wife being one of them. Crystal knew I had a crush on her. I also began to accuse her of being unfaithful. The arguments increased and increased until something happened, Crystal became pregnant. I was fourteen and she was fifteen. What were we going to do?

She wanted to keep the baby but I was scared to

death. Crystal told her mother and she told me to tell mines. There was no way in hell that I was going to tell my mother that. She would kill me. I kept telling Crystal that I would tell my mother, but I never did. So one day while at home, a knock was at the door. When I went to open the door, to my surprise it was Crystal and her mother standing there. My heart dropped. My mom asked who was at the door. I told her that it was Crystal and her mother, and that they were there to speak to her. After I let them in the house, I went straight to my room. There was some loud arguing and after a short while both Crystal and her mother left. My mother did not believe that it was my baby. She said I was too young to make a child. Little did she know that even if her son could not make a child, he sure was practicing a lot in her house while she was at work.

    Nine months passed and Crystal eventually gave birth to our beautiful baby girl. As soon as she came out, there would be no denying that she was mines. That child looked exactly like me. From early on I took on my responsibility as a father. I would keep my daughter every weekend. During that time when I had my daughter, Crystal began to go out more. She was frequenting the teen clubs a lot while I was at home with our daughter. I frequented the teen clubs as well, but I got real jealous when she would go. Those insecurities began to fester inside of me.

    One night Crystal went out as usual but I just got a bad feeling about that night. My intuition kept telling me that something was wrong. I waited until I knew that she would be home and called her house. I kept calling and calling her phone, but the line was busy. There was no call waiting back then so if you were on the phone the line would stay busy. I just knew that she was on the phone with another guy. I called that number for about three hours straight. Love will make you do crazy things. I eventually got tired and went to bed.

The next day Crystal called me and said she met someone and was breaking up with me. I begged, pleaded, and cried for her to stay with me. It did not seem to faze her. Her mind was made up and she was done with me. My heart felt heavy. It felt like someone stabbed me in my chest. I had never felt like that before in my life. The world seemed different. I had no appetite. I could not sleep. All I could think about was how she was with someone else and how she left me. I am not going to even lie; I contemplated killing myself and her. I did not know how to make that pain go away.

I began using my daughter as leverage against her. I would not pick my daughter up when it was my turn to keep her. I would just make it hard for her to go out. I was bitter and it showed. I just could not understand why she did not love me anymore. I felt as if I lucked up finding her and now that she was gone, no one else would want me. My self-esteem and confidence was at an all-time low. Heartbreak is one of the worst feelings one can inflict on a person.

I would just go to school and come home to sleep. I isolated myself from the world. My mother tried to console me but she could not take that pain away. Crystal had a new boyfriend and I was all alone. That did not seem fair.

Why did I ever have to meet her? What was the cure to this dreadful ailment of heartbreak? At that young age, I learned a valuable lesson. The cure was time. I began to hang out with my friends. I got out of the house more. When you are going through heartbreak, one of the worst things you can do is to be alone. You want to be alone, but it does not help. In the beginning it is good to take a little time for you but you must get out and socialize after a while.

    I hung out with my friends and I began to talk to different girls. They were actually talking back to me. My confidence began to rise and I became a little player. I can even admit that out of the group of friends that I hung out with, I was not the best looking. Amazingly, I got the most females. My personality and confidence went a long way. It was a numbers game to me. If I attempted to talk to ten females, I would probably get one real phone number. That was just fine with me. It meant that I had to hustle and get those numbers.

    Eventually I got over Crystal. My heart got broken, but it healed. I made it through it and if you are experiencing heartbreak you will make it through as well. There is no cheating the pain though. You cannot screw, drink, eat, or sleep your way from the pain. The only prescription is time and it shall pass. Crystal and I did try to get back together a little later on but it never worked. I even proposed to her, unfortunately she pawned my ring. That is a story for another day.

THE ADVERSITIES IN OUR PAST MAKE US STRONGER FOR THE ONES IN OUR FUTURE.

Chapter 5

The Molested III

"You don't drown by falling into water. You drown by staying there."
~Anonymous

I first met Gina while I was still in high school. I believe I was a sophomore and she was a senior. She did not attend the same school as me. We met while at the Martin Luther King Jr. Parade. My friends and I were on the prowl to see who got the most numbers from females that day. If I remember correctly, I got about six numbers that day making me the winner. Only two of the numbers worked, Gina's number being one of them.

We hit it off real good. She was beautiful and she drove so that was a plus. We would spend countless hours talking on the phone. One night we talked for about five hours straight, neither one of us wanting to hang up the phone. Those were the days. She was even cool about me having a child. Most girls I met back then did not really want to talk to me once they found out I had a child. Gina was different though.

We began to get real close and Gina disclosed to me one day that her stepfather was molesting her. I could not believe it. Being a teenager, I did not really grasp the magnitude of what that really meant. One day while I was at home, I got a call from Gina. She was crying hysterically. Gina informed me that she was home alone with her stepfather. I did not know what to do. She just wanted me to stay on the phone with her as she cried. Gina was so scared to be alone in the house with him. He never did anything to her that day, probably because she was on the phone with me. I just stayed on the phone with her. Neither one of us said anything while on the phone. She just wanted me to stay on the phone with her until her mother came home. After about one hour of us being on the phone, her mother finally came home. I will never forget that experience. I had never heard anybody that frightened in my life.

Gina and I would date for a few months but we were forced to break up. Her mother found out that I had a daughter and felt that I was too experienced for Gina. Even though we broke up, we remained good friends. Being that I always remembered what she disclosed to me when we were teenagers, I asked her if she would share her story with me for my book. She agreed with no problem.

From what she can remember, the molestations began when she was around eight years old. Her mother got married to her stepfather when she was about seven years old. The first year of having a stepfather was actually good. He seemed real caring and provided her with the love that she had not received from her real father. As soon as she turned eight, things started to change.

Her stepfather would come into her room while she was asleep and would remove the covers off of her. He would then turn on the television and watch it as he sat on her bed. He did that for a couple of weeks and Gina thought nothing of it. Her stepfather then began to pull her underwear to the side and fondle her. This would cause Gina to awake. When she looked around, he would act as if he was watching the television. Gina was unsure if she was imagining this or not. He would continue to fondle her while she slept. Being so young, I can only imagine what was going through her head when she awoke to being fondled.

After a few incidents, he stopped pretending as if he was watching television when she would catch him. When he was done molesting her, he told her not to tell her mother because it would make her upset. Being that she did not want to get her mother upset, she kept the secret for a while. He would continue to fondle her each night as she slept. After a few months, Gina felt that she should tell her mother. She actually got the courage and told her mother what was being done to her by her stepfather.

Gina's mother was furious when Gina told her what her stepfather had been doing to her at night. She immediately packed up all of their belongings and moved in with Gina's grandfather. Her grandfather inquired as to why they were moving in, but Gina's mother did not want to tell him because he would have killed that man. Gina's stepfather begged and pleaded for them to come back. He actually confessed to Gina's mother what he had done and even promised not to ever do it again. Gina's mother then asked her if she wanted to press charges. She told Gina that if charges were pressed that Gina would have to go to court and testify about what happened to her. Gina told her mother that she did not want to go in front of all those people and tell them what happened.

I have known Gina for over twenty years now, and I have even met her mother. She is a very nice woman. What she did back then by asking her daughter that question was devastating. No child would want to go in front of a courtroom and tell the horrors of what happened to them. Many parents would pray that their child comes to them and disclose if someone was harming them so they could protect them. Gina's mother should have called the police, not ask her daughter if she wanted to press charges. I do not know if she did not believe her, but you cannot take chances like that.

A week after they moved out, Gina and her mother moved back in with her stepfather. With the promise that he would not touch her again, Gina thought she was safe. Unfortunately after a few months, her stepfather began fondling her again. This continued for a few years and Gina told her mother once again that she was being fondled. Gina's mother and stepfather argued for a few days but they did not move out that time. She does not know what was being said to her mother but no action was being taken. Since nothing was being done and Gina not knowing anything about sex, she just went along with the nightly fondling. It was not until she began hearing friends of hers describing how similar things were happening to them that she realized that what was being done to her was not right. In March of 1995 was the last time the molestation occurred. Gina was a senior in high school and she had enough. She made it up in her mind that her stepfather would never touch her again. She packed up her stuff and moved in with her grandfather.

When we fast forward to the present time, Gina is a mother of three handsome boys and one beautiful daughter. She works in sales and is very successful. This woman is a hustler. She could sell an Eskimo ice while in an igloo. She is good at what she does. With regards to her mother, Gina felt resentment towards her for a very long time. Since she has been going to church, she has let go of a lot of resentment that she held against her mother. She has finally forgiven her mother for not protecting her. For a long time Gina would wonder if her mother ever believed her about being touched. Even though her stepfather confessed to doing it, Gina just felt that her mother did not believe it happened. Gina even questioned did her mother even love her. She does not feel that she has gotten closure about her mother's lack of action in protecting her, but she is content with not bringing it up with her mother.

With regards to her relationships, being molested had a big impact on her life. It took Gina many years to ever climax from intercourse. It was very difficult for her to let go. If her mates would try to have sex with her while she was asleep, she would awake and physically attack them. Gina found herself looking for love in all the wrong places. This has led to many failed relationships. As I am writing this, I can remember one time when we were dating we got into a big argument. The argument got very heated. All of a sudden Gina began to cry and tremble; she would not say a word to me. It was as if she was in shock. No matter what I did to get a response from her, it did not work. I took her to my house and laid her in my bed to rest. After a few hours she awoke as if nothing ever happened. We never talked about what happened that day but I think she could have been having a flashback of her being molested. I was just confused about the whole situation.

When it comes to Gina's stepfather, he is still around today and she still communicates with him. She ensures that she never leaves her kids alone with him. Surprisingly, about two years ago her stepfather came to her and asked her for forgiveness. He confessed to her what he had done and that he was very sorry. A rush of emotions came over her as she cried. Gina would have never thought in a million years that the man who had ruined her childhood was now apologizing and asking her for forgiveness. She believed that he was truly sincere with his apology, so she forgave him. She believes by doing so, gave her a sense of closure. To have him admit to what he did and to beg for forgiveness was something she never thought would ever happen.

Recently Gina's stepfather had a heart attack. He made it through it and Gina went to visit him in the hospital to make sure he was alright. She felt that his heart attack was justice for what he had done to her. She does not wish death upon him and she would even cry if he passed away. She just felt as if he got a little payback for what he put her through.

Even though Gina got more closure than most, the wounds will always be there. Sometimes kids in situations like Gina's have to turn to help outside the house. Her mother that was supposed to protect her was no help to her when she needed her the most. Gina made a conscious effort to overcome what was done to her. She could have used it as an excuse to not succeed in life but she did not. It is an everyday battle but Gina fights through and does the best she can to survive. I always tell people that when you are a small child and people find out that you are having a tough childhood, they feel sorry for you. Unfortunately, when you become an adult, no one cares about your past. We all have one. What are you going to do with the cards that you are dealt? You can either fold, or play that hand. Gina chose to play that hand, will you.

SOMETIMES YOU JUST HAVE TO TAKE AN HONEST LOOK AT THE SITUATION THAT YOU ARE IN AND DECIDE THAT YOU WANT TO MAKE A CHANGE.

Chapter 6

The Felon

"Nothing great has ever been achieved except by those who dared to believe that something inside them was superior to circumstances."
~Bruce Barton

When it comes to dealing with adversity, I think Richard has had his share for a lifetime. Richard is dating a family member of mines so I have gotten to know him for quite some time now. When I first met him, I was informed that he had spent ten years in prison. Naturally I was cautious as to who this guy really was. When we had discussions, it was clear that he had done some time in prison. He would ask me a lot of questions regarding simple social things that most people should know. If you did not know he had done time, you would assume that he may not be intelligent, but Richard is one of the smartest people I know. He would question anything he did not understand or if he wanted clarification on something.

Since Richard served time in prison, naturally he was prejudged. He was prejudged by my family, he was prejudged by police, and he was prejudged by society. With all these prejudgments, how does he continue? It is pure determination. Richard is dark skinned, tall and has aggressive mannerisms. Even with all these things, he can be placed in any environment and fit right in. I have seen him in settings with white people, black people, and even law enforcement and he fits right in. He has this quality about him that allows him to adapt to any situation.

So how did he end up in prison for ten years? Well, he committed various crimes in which he was caught and arrested for. There was a deeper issue though that started him on that life of crime, and it is an interesting one. Growing up, Richard came from a two parent household. Once again, where we come from that was not a common thing. A broken family and poverty was the blueprint in our neighborhood. Not only were his mother and father in the same household, they were actually married. This was another anomaly in our neighborhood. His parents were very well off. They were educated people who provided everything to their kids as well as teaching them morals and ethics.

On the outside, his childhood was as perfect as one could ask for, but on the inside something else was going on with Richard. He was bullied and made fun of by his peers. Richard's teeth protruded out a little more than others so the kids would really get on him about that. As adults we may look at that as innocent teasing, but as a young child bullying and teasing can affect a child for life. Richard tried to combat their bullying by giving them money so they would be friends with him. It worked a few times, but for the most part they just continued with the bullying. Richard just wanted to be accepted by his peers, but he was denied their friendship. Richard's life of crime began with him stealing pencils in the third grade to please the other kids. The seeds were being planted for a life of crime and hardship and he did not even know it.

When Richard became a teenager, his low self-esteem and lack of confidence had him looking for acceptance anywhere. He was finally accepted by Ted, a local teen who was already dabbling into the criminal world. When you have a void in your life, the right or wrong person can fill it up. Unfortunately for Richard, Ted was the wrong person to fill the void he had in his life at that point.

Richard and Ted began committing burglaries. Ted had already been doing it prior to meeting Richard, so now he had a partner in crime. They would break into people's houses while the homeowners were at work. Ted did not have much, so he was content with the little things they found in the houses, such as electronics and petty cash. Richard on the other hand came from money so he was used to nice things. He wanted more than what they were stealing. He wanted jewelry, safes, and other valuables that would require more of a risk. Richard's ambition had him burglarizing houses at all hours, day and night. He was relishing in his new found acceptance, no matter the consequences.

As with everything in life, if you do something long enough, you are bound to get good at it (whether legal or illegal). Richard became a good criminal. He escalated his criminal resume from burglarizing houses while the occupants were at work, to engaging in home invasions with everyone inside. Richard stopped burglarizing the homes of working people. They kind of reminded him of his parents. He figured why should he take what they worked hard for. Richard began burglarizing the homes of drug dealers. He had no problems stealing from criminals. With that thought process Richard kind of reminded me of Omar from *The Wire*, except Richard was not gay. He was kicking doors in and tying everyone up who was inside. He would usually get the safes, or stashes without incident. To the few who did not comply, they quickly learned the consequences of their mistakes.

Richard was getting money, running away from home, and overall being a menace to society. Unfortunately, his luck soon ran out and he began to get arrested. The first time he went to jail he was scared but after he saw what it was it about, it was no longer a deterrence to his life of crime. He was too far gone. His mother would scold and pray for him to change, but it had no effect on him. Eventually the revolving door of him going in and out of jail came to an end. He was convicted on numerous counts of burglary and robbery charges. Richard was sentenced to seventeen years in prison.

For most people that would have been a hard pill to swallow, but not Richard. He was tired, or rather exhausted of his life of crime. Mentally he had accepted those seventeen years. He did not even think about him being locked up for that long. He was more concerned on why was he the way he was. Richard knew that if he did not figure this out, when he was released he would be right back in prison.

In the beginning of him serving his time, naturally

he began to lash out and cause problems. Richard was selling marijuana in prison and "hustling". He acquired a locker full of goods. In prison, this put you at an elite status. One day Richard went to the restroom to masturbate, this was a common practice in prison. The inmates would sit on the toilet and look at porn magazines while they masturbated. While Richard was handling his "business", he just suddenly stopped and made a realization. He was on a toilet masturbating in prison. This could not be what his life had come to. Richard was used to having sex with multiple women anytime he wanted to. This got him real depressed for a long time.

After a while of being depressed and getting nowhere with his rebellious behavior in prison, Richard found out about a program being given in the prison called "Hope Restored". This program put him on a path to restoring his life. It was run by Basil Phillips. The program was given to inmates who volunteered to be a part of it. It did not reduce their time nor did it promise to have any sway with the courts. The program was for those inmates who were tired of their behaviors and wanted to truly change.

Richard was taught in the program that he was living a lie. He was not created that way that he was behaving. When his mother held him up as a baby and everyone looked at him, they said look at that baby boy, not look at that criminal. Something in his childhood caused the criminal behavior. For Richard, it was not being accepted and being bullied. That caused him to put up wall after wall to protect his hurt feelings and that little child inside. So as an adult, there was an impenetrable fortress protecting him.

The program required the inmates to be humble. The inmates were all given nick names while they were in the program. The nick names given to them centered on their perceived flaws. Richard was called the buck tooth rabbit because of his protruding teeth. That did not sit well with him. He had been bullied because of his teeth as a young child, so now all the other inmates were going to call him the buck tooth rabbit as his new nick name in the program. It was hard at first for him to accept, but it was a method to the madness as he would soon find out. Some of the other inmates were made to stand in trash cans as toilet paper rolls were launched at them. The idea behind all that was to create humility among the inmates. Once humility was created, the inmates could be open to listening and ultimately changing.

There were robbers, drug dealers, and killers all in this program. The program called for them to explore their childhoods and to ultimately get a better understanding on what went wrong in their lives. As soon as that realization could be made, the healing could begin. Richard did well in the program, but at one point he ended up getting kicked out of it. After being out the program for a few weeks, Richard felt as something was missing. He quickly begged to get back into the program. Richard was eventually accepted back into the program. He knew that this program would save his life. After weeks of being in the program, Richard graduated from it without any other problems. Even after graduating, Richard still had to use the skills he learned in the program to finish off the rest of his sentence successfully, and ultimately his life.

When Richard first got into prison he began using cocaine, a habit which he had done out in the streets. Not too long after he graduated the Hope Restored program something happened that let Richard know that he was really changing. One day while out in the yard with another inmate, they began snorting cocaine. This was something that he and that inmate did on a daily basis. Something was different, it did not feel the same to him. In that moment Richard made a realization that he was a junkie. He did cocaine when he was out of prison and he was still doing cocaine while in prison.

God spoke to him in that moment and told him to close his hands. If he kept his hands open, cocaine would always find its way to him. Richard gave the inmate the rest of his cocaine and told him that he was done. That was something that you just did not do in prison. You would never give anything away for free. He could have sold the rest of the cocaine, but Richard was done. The inmate asked him several times if he was sure that he did not want anything for it, but Richard never wavered. He never did cocaine again. The mind is a powerful thing. Sometimes you just have to take an honest look at the situation that you are in and decide that you want to make a change.

After ten years of being incarcerated, Richard was released early from that seventeen year sentence. Richard was finally a free man. He ended up getting a good job with a manufacturing company and makes good money. He has a handsome son, who he cherishes and mentors daily.

Richard made a conscious effort to change his situation. He did not let that adversity get the best of him. He vows never to go back to the street life or prison. He equates the experience of the streets to a carnival that you have been to a million times. He knows what to expect and knows what comes with it. There is no interest in that carnival for him anymore. His new passion is raising his son and being a good boyfriend.

    The adversity of incarceration was conquered by Richard through prayer, a program, and him just being tired. If you are unfortunate enough to be in this situation, just know that you can get through it. It is never too late to make that change.

GOD IS LOVE AND LOVE IS GOD.

Chapter 7

The Religion

"We are not human beings having a spiritual experience. We are spiritual beings having a human experience."
~Pierre Teilhard de Chardin

    The topic of religion is a very sensitive one to many people around the world. Many people have been killed and persecuted over the subject. When it comes to my own personal beliefs, they do not coincide with what the masses believe. They definitely do not align with what I was taught or raised up on. But before I go deep into that, let me start off with my upbringing on religion.

    From as far back as I can remember we were not a religious family. My mom was just living her life. She was arrested once in Bahamas before I was born and as she would put it, she was a little wild back in the day. She was no joke. Today she is the kindest woman in the world. Sometimes too kind, if one can actually be too kind.

    When I was around six or seven years old my family began going to a Catholic Church. The Catholic Church was very big. I remember the loud church bells ringing every hour on the hour. You could hear those church bells all throughout the neighborhood. From the little that I do remember from that church, it had a somber feeling to it. Then again, I was a small child; I had no understanding of that place at that time. The people that came there were dressed very nice and it seemed to run in an orderly fashion. We did not attend that church long, so I do not really remember learning anything specific about religion there.

After we left that church, we began going to a Jamaican church, which was more of a Baptist Church. I actually liked going to that church. I was a little older so I could remember more about that church. The church had a kids' Sunday School Session in which we sang songs and learned various stories from the bible. As I type this, memories of me singing *"Father Abraham"* and *"Jesus Loves Me"* pop up in my head. The majority of my childhood religious foundation came from this church. I was introduced to the concept of heaven and hell for the first time. From what I heard, I definitely did not want to go to hell.

Unfortunately, we left that church because we moved to a new area and the church was too far. We began going to a Haitian Church. It was a Baptist Church as well. My mom was Haitian so naturally she felt more comfortable at this church among her people. I on the other hand, did not like it. The majority, if not all of the services were in Creole. I understood Creole, but not *this* Creole. It was as if they were speaking ancient Creole. They were also very strict there. If you did not follow the rules they had there as a child, you were getting disciplined. This was back in the days, so anybody could hit anyone's child and it was all good. That would definitely not fly today.

Since I did not like this church, I did not want to go. We had a church van that would pick us up every Sunday before service. I would purposely take my time getting dressed. I would hide my shoes the night before so I could not find them or I would blatantly cry so I could not go. My mother was not having that. If we missed that church van, she would beat me and we would take the bus. I remember one Sunday, I began my stall tactics like usual. I hid my church shoes and purposely delayed taking a bath. My mom told me if I did not take a bath in five minutes, that she was going to beat the hell out of me. At that age I did not like taking baths so I thought I would outsmart her. I went into the bathroom and just ran the water for about ten minutes. I wet my face so it looked good. As soon as I exited the bathroom, my mom went in after me. She came right back out and asked did I take a bath. Of course I lied and told her I did. At that moment she held the bone dry bar of soap in her hand, pointing it at me. I knew I was done. My mom beat me and gave me a bath at the same time. After all that drama that I caused, we still made it to church that Sunday.

I would continue to go unwillingly to church until I was a teenager. By then I was too rebellious and my mom was tired of fighting with me on everything else so she did not push going to church anymore. Once I became an adult I had enough of a religious foundation to live my life. I would pray every morning and night. I believed that there was a devil and he was constantly trying to corrupt us. I also believed that if I did not live my life a certain way, then I would not go to heaven. As I got older, I began to question many things about this "religion" thing. I began with the bible. I had read the bible from time to time so I was familiar with it. By no means was I a religious professor of the bible but I had general knowledge of it. How did this book come about? I never really thought about where it came from. I thought that God just dropped it here on earth for us, I soon found out that was not exactly the case.

Before I continue, to those of you who are very religious some of my views and thoughts may come off as blasphemous. My purpose in this chapter is to share my battle with my religious and spiritual beliefs, not to offend anyone on what they believe in.

With regards to the creation of bible, I found out that there were many prophets and authors that had scriptures floating around for thousands of years. Eventually councils such as Laodicea and Nicaea, to name a few, were formed throughout history to address different gospels in the bible. These councils consisted of hundreds of the most respected bishops and religious personnel. In these councils they voted on the direction of Christianity and specifically which gospels would be included in the bible. There are many lost gospels, such as *The Gospel of Mary, The Revelation of Peter, and The Book of Enoch,* to name a few. For whatever reason, many of these lost gospels were not voted in. For me, just thinking logically I had a problem with that. It made me think that all the information was not provided to me. The premise that the creation of this book was left up to man to vote what went in or not made it seem flawed.

I really struggled with that for a long time. What else was being kept from me? I lost my faith in religion. I wondered did I even need to pray. Was God even listening to me? What would happen if I stopped praying? I used to pray every morning and night, so one day I stopped doing it. I reflected back on my many times of struggle and praying for help and it never came. I became somewhat of an atheist. I still believed in a creator, but he/she was not paying attention as to what was going on in this world. Innocent kids were being killed. There was poverty and hunger all over the world. They were also warring countries which resulted in countless deaths. With all that suffering in pain going on in this world, why was God not helping? Yep, I was convinced we were on our own.

My family was still religious, so I had to keep my new found lack of faith in religion to myself. Whenever we were together during a holiday meal and a prayer was being said over the meal, I would bow my head but keep my eyes open. I did that wherever I went and there was a prayer taking place. I just truly did not see the purpose of prayer anymore, I was so lost. It is kind of funny because as my eyes were open during those prayers, I would see other people's eyes open as well. Did they lose faith in religion as well?

My life was going just fine without prayer and religion. I was living more righteous than many people who went to church faithfully. I can remember getting into many discussions with friends on why I did not need to go to church. Many women stopped dating me after they found out about my view on religion. They felt like they wanted a godly man, and I did not fit that mold. After many years of feeling like this, and thinking that I had everything figured out, I came across some videos on YouTube of this woman named Reverend Valerie Love. Now let me tell you this, watching those videos changed my life. This woman was inspiring. She was a self-proclaimed Christian Witch. I had never heard of such a thing. As I researched more about her, I came to know of her story. She lived as a Jehovah Witness for over twenty years. She was truly committed to the religion. Fortunately, something in her spirit was pushing her to go further than where she was being a Jehovah Witness.

    Reverend Valerie Love broke many of the rules that the Jehovah Witnesses had in place. She was eventually banished from the community. This is when her eyes were truly opened. She used the banishment as a time to explore different religions. Reverend Valerie Love spent time with Muslims, Jews, and Christians alike, to name a few. She talked, ate, and prayed with them all. This was something that she would have never thought of doing as a Jehovah Witness. Through all of her years of travelling and studying different religions after being a Jehovah Witness, she noticed one simple thing. Every one of those religions were preaching love. It did not matter what religion it was, love could be felt in each one of them. It came down to this simple premise, God is love.

    That simple statement changed my way of thinking. I was so caught up on what this religion was saying or what that religion was saying, that I missed the simple message of God is love. In my view, religion is like the middle man between you and God. Some people need that middle man, so they enjoy religion. There is no judgment from me on that. I choose to connect with God myself, without the middleman of religion. I can appreciate many things from religions all around the world. I just choose not to subscribe to anything dealing with hate.

Since God is love and love is God, hate can be nowhere in that equation. I will give you an example of something that I was confused about with regards to something in the bible I read. In Exodus 20:5, it says, "….that I, the Lord, your God, am a jealous God." How can God be jealous? That does not resonate with me. The creator of our world and the universe has a human emotion of jealousy, I could not understand how that could be. I guess the premise of that verse was that God only wanted us worshiping him(or her). I just had a big issue with the use of the word jealous and associating it with God. Also, for those people that are homosexual, is it their fate to burn in" hell" because of their sexuality? I just cannot wrap my head around that. I have talked to many people who are homosexual and they have expressed that they were born that way. Nothing traumatic happened to them. Around the age that I began to like the opposite sex, they began liking the same sex. Who am I to judge them? It is my belief that the bible is not to be taken literally but metaphysically and allegorically. I believe we have to look deep inside of the messages that are in it to truly understand what was trying to be relayed to us.

At this present time I have no issues with praying or partaking in any prayer sessions. I will go to church with anyone who invites me. It can be a Muslim, Jew, or Christian. As long as love is being preached, then I am cool with that. If there is any place where people are gathered and the message of love is being preached, then it is a good place to be. I choose not to get caught up in the semantics of the many religions anymore. This adversity with religion was a tough but rewarding journey for me. I was able to truly be at peace with my spirituality. Although my views may not be your views, I challenge anyone who is questioning their faith to seek out the answers. Do not be afraid to ask questions. You were created as an intelligent being to seek and gain knowledge, not be a blinded follower. If any religion that you are a part of discourages you from asking questions, then that should be a red flag. I do not claim to have all the answers, nor do I think anyone on earth does either. I just know what feels right within my spirit. Look deep within your spirit and the answers you seek shall be answered for you as well as they were for me.

SOMETIMES YOU HAVE TO FACE FEAR HEAD ON, GIVING IT YOUR ALL.

Chapter 8

The Recruit

"Believe you can and you're halfway there." ~Theodore Roosevelt

During my senior year in high school, I had no idea what I wanted to do when I graduated. I did know one thing; I did not want to go to college. I was tired of school; a break was the top priority on my list. It was not as if I was not smart enough to go to college, I was just lazy. I graduated number thirty-two out of a class of five hundred and twenty. That was not bad for someone who was barely even trying. I did not take an ACT or SAT test. I did however take the Armed Services Vocational Aptitude Battery (ASVAB). This was a multiple choice test given to students in high school by the military to let you know what skills you were good at. If you decided to go into the military, they would use your ASVAB scores to determine what job you would have while serving.

Since I was not going to college, I decided to go to the military. My brother was already in the Army at the time so I did not want to go there. I could not swim, so the Navy and the Coast Guard were out of the question. That left the National Guard, Air Force, and The Marine Corps. My life had been nothing but tough up to that point, so I wanted to go somewhere easy. I chose the Marines. I know what you all are thinking, the Marines, there is nothing easy about that. I had no idea what I was getting into.

My recruiter was great. I have to give it up to the Marine Corps. They have some of the best recruiters in the military. They have to be the best because recruiting young adults to chose the Marine Corps over the other military branches was a tough gig. Since I scored really high on my ASVAB, I was an attractive potential recruit to them. My recruiter sold me on the dream of being the best of the best. He did not say it was going to be a cake walk, but he never told me I was in for the toughest challenge of my life at that time. The Marine Corps is the smallest branch in the military but by far the toughest. The basic training was even longer than the other military branches. I believed that I was up for the challenge of becoming a Marine at that time so I decided to enlist. Before I knew it, I graduated high school and was on my way to Parris Island, South Carolina for twelve weeks of hell at The United States Marine Corps Boot Camp.

When I first arrived there, it went just as you saw in the movies. There were scary Drill Instructors yelling at us to do various things that we could not do right. For the first three days there was no sleep. When I say no sleep, I am not exaggerating; your eyes could not close. We went from an assembly line of getting numerous medical shots to dental exams, to getting shaved bald. If you have never gone without sleep for three days, I do not recommend it. You begin to hallucinate after about the second day. I began to wonder why in the hell did I sign up for this. Throughout my time as a recruit in boot camp I faced many adversities. I could write a book on my whole boot camp experience alone, but I will only discuss a few.

One of the toughest things I had to do while in boot camp was learn how to swim. Even though I was from South Florida, I never learned how to swim. I went to the beach and pool many times while I was home, I just never went deep into the water. In order to become a Marine, you need to know how to swim. My recruiter knew that I did not know how to swim, but he told me that I would learn while in boot camp. If I only knew what was in store for me with regards to learning how to swim, things may have turned out differently.

Our swim qualification training was one week long. After that, if you did not pass within that week, you had to leave the platoon you had been with for all those weeks. You had to move into the barracks of a new platoon that was not as far along as your old platoon was with regards to training and participate in another week of swim qualifications. This meant that you had to finish off boot camp with the new platoon that you were with. Being that the swim qualifications was at the halfway mark of boot camp, you were already bonded with your platoon. No one wanted to go to a new platoon. This was also a big deal because the move to a new platoon meant that your graduation date was pushed back. Family and friends had already made arrangements for specific dates to come your graduation. So besides being embarrassing, it was a burden on your loved ones to change that date. So basically what all that meant was that I could not fail the swim qualifications.

The first day of swim qualifications had finally come and I was so nervous. There were about a hundred recruits waiting at the edge of the pool waiting to begin the test. The first part of the swim qualifications consisted of swimming twenty-five meters, while wearing your full military uniform. You could not use any techniques which caused your hands to come out of the water. I really did not have a chance. The Drill Instructor yelled go and we all jumped in. Naturally, I failed miserably. Only about thirty of us failed that first part. The rest of the recruits moved on to the other parts of the qualification while we stayed stuck at the first part.

The funny thing about the thirty recruits that failed was that we were all of color. Black people not being able to swim may be a stereotype, but it was looking pretty true in boot camp. The Drill Instructor that was tasked with teaching us how to pass the first part was a male and he was mean. He taught us the backstroke and we had to practice that technique from about ten in the morning to about five in the evening. Needless to say, that first day was an epic failure. I was dog tired and was really stressing. I never learned how to swim and there was no way that I was going to pass this swim qualification in one week.

The second day came and it was the same. We all had to practice that back stroke until we passed those twenty-five meters. Little by little those recruits that were confident attempted it. Some made it, while others did not. Our group of minority non-swimmers was down to about twenty. I kept trying but kept falling short about five to ten meters. The day was coming to an end and a few more recruits passed on to the other part of the swim qualification. Day two was not my day either. When I went back to the barracks, I was exhausted. I had been attempting this twenty-five meter test for two straight days. There was no way I was going to have energy for day three. That night all I dreamed about was being in that water and swimming. It was so bad that I awoke to doing the backstroke in my bed in the middle of the night. Passing that swim qualification was really bothering me.

    The third day came and I told myself that I was going to pass this thing today. I remember talking to God and begging him to please help me pass that test. I talked to God a lot in boot camp. It is kind of funny because when everything was good, God did not hear from me. But in my time of need, we were best friends. I had attempted the test about ten times that day and was still coming up short about ten meters. On try number eleven, I had put it into my head that this was going to be my last time trying. I was going to pass it. I was going to dig deep and give it my all. If that meant that I was going to keep swimming until I passed out or hit my head on the wall, then so be it.

    As attempt number eleven began, I can remember that I started off fast and strong. But all the other times I started off fast and strong as well. Once I was about fifteen meters in, my arms began to feel like they were on fire. I was not going to stop; they would have to just fall off. I just keep swimming and swimming. All of a sudden, I felt a hard thump. I was so much into the zone of swimming that at first I did not know what the thump was. After a few seconds I realized what the thump was. It was the back of my head hitting the wall. I had finally made it. I actually swam twenty-five meters. I was so excited. I could not believe it, a kid from the inner city just learned how to swim.

    Unfortunately, my victory parade was cut short. I had only passed the first part of the swim qualification. There were four more parts. The next part of the test consisted of treading water for about four minutes. Those twenty-five meters was one thing but treading water was the real deal. My swimming skills were not prepared for this. I was so tired. I had just spent three days trying to swim twenty-five meters, now I had to tread water for four minutes. I did not sign up for all of that.

    For the treading water part of the test, I got a female Drill Instructor. Boy was I happy for that. I was used to seeing just men for six weeks, so to see a pretty female in a bathing suit was a gift. Even though she was mean and a Marine, but a female nonetheless.

    She began by taking me to the deep end of the pool. I was still close enough to the edge that if I panicked, I could grab a hold. I would tread water for about thirty seconds and grab the side of the pool. I did that about two times. The female Drill Instructor told me that if I grabbed the side of the pool one more time, she was going to drag me out to the middle of the pool where I could not grab anything. So what did I do on my next attempt to tread water, I panicked after thirty seconds and grabbed the side of the pool again. I thought to myself that I was not going to drown in that pool, they had me messed up. As promised, the female Drill Instructor grabbed me by my collar and dragged me to the middle of the pool. She then instructed me to begin treading water. It would be real this time. I no longer had the side of the pool to grab onto if I panicked. So I began to tread water for about forty-five seconds, when the fear and panic took over. There was no side of the pool to grab. I began to flail my arms trying to stay afloat, but it was not working. I began to sink deep into the pool. That female Drill Instructor was not even trying to help me.

    I fought and I fought but I could not break the surface of the pool. Many thoughts came to mind at that time. I wondered why did I just not go to college. Why did I enlist in the Marine Corps? After flailing for what felt like an eternity, something strange happened. I stopped fighting. I thought to myself at that moment, I am going to die. This lady was really going to let me die. I can truly say that I accepted death at that moment. I put both of my hands out to my side as if I was on a cross and tilted my head back. I began to descend deeper and deeper in the pool. There was a euphoric calmness in the acceptance of what I thought was death. All of a sudden, I felt someone grab me by my collar and pull me out of the pool. It was the female Drill Instructor. She called me an idiot and said that I was going to tread water until I got it right. The amazing thing was that I treaded water again the next time for the full four minutes without any issues. I finished and passed the rest of the swim qualifications without any problems. The final part of the swim qualifications consisted of me jumping off of a twenty foot platform into the deep end of the pool with my full uniform on and swimming safely to the side of the pool. That was actually fun. I was so proud that I was able to accomplish that.

Why did I pass the rest of my swim qualifications with ease? The answer is simple, my fear was gone. Once that female Drill Instructor left me in that water to drown, I had accepted death. The fear of drowning was no longer a concern because in my mind I had already drowned. The adversity of going through Marine Corps boot camp was one of the toughest challenges of my life but I overcame it. Specifically when it came to passing the swimming qualification, I was my own worst enemy. The doubt and fear took over and manifested into me failing. Once I eliminated those two things from my mind, success was instant. Sometimes you have to face fear head on, giving it your all. Defeat is always a possibility, but that is none of your concern. Focus your energy on prevailing and that too shall manifest itself for you as it did with me. Be brave.

WE ARE ALL HERE
ON BORROWED TIME.
MAKE YOUR TIME
HERE MEANINGFUL.

Chapter 9
The Drug Dealer

"I am not a victim. I am an angry survivor."
~Nina Bawden

When I was growing up, I had a childhood friend named Ricky. I met Ricky through one of my cousins. Me and my cousins had a rap group at the time called "*Sak Pase*", which basically means what's up in Creole. We recorded one song and auditioned for a talent show. As with most groups, we did not last long. We were recording at one of the producer's girlfriend house at the time. She got tired of us coming in and out her house, so that was the end of our rap group. Soon after that I met Ricky. We used to always discuss our dreams with each other. I was going to be a big rapper making lots of money, while Ricky was going to rap and produce as well. We were young and full of big ideas and dreams. Who knew how life would steer us in very different paths from each other.

Ricky was a Seven Day Advantest. This meant that his family observed Saturday as their Sabbath. So from Friday at sunset to Saturday at sunset, Ricky was stuck at home with his family. Being a male teenager full of testosterone, this was a struggle for Ricky on the weekends. The weekends were the time where we were looking to sow our wild oats. Since Ricky was stuck at home for the majority of the weekend, he would miss out on the many rendezvous with various females that we had lined up.

Since Ricky could not hang out on the weekend, we tried to hang out with each other during the week day. I can remember one school night during the week, Ricky had a bright idea that we should go to the nudist beach to see some naked women. At that age, what male teenager did not want to see naked women. It was kind of late, but we decided that we would not be there long. We did not have a car so we had to ride the public bus. On the bus ride all we could think about was all the fine naked women we would see. We did live in South Florida, so beautiful women were all around us.

As soon as we got off the bus, we hit the beach on a mission. We searched up and down that beach for naked women. Unfortunately, all we saw was naked old men. I was so mad with Ricky. He had hyped me up that we were going to see beautiful naked women. He even told me that he had been there before and that he saw lots of them. We came all that way to see droopy scrotum sacks. By this time it was already midnight and all the buses had stopped running. We were stuck on the beach with no ride back. Luckily an out of service bus passed by us and the driver felt sorry for us and gave us a ride back.

I ended up going to boot camp, while Ricky stayed at home. He was working two jobs just barely making ends meet. Ricky began wondering why was he working so hard when he could make money the fast way. He decided that he was going to become a drug dealer. Ricky saw many of the local drug dealers in the area making quick money, while he had to slave at two jobs. He was tired. Ricky always had a fascination with drug dealers and that life in general. He decided that not only was he going to sell drugs, he was going to do it the smart way. Ricky saw where all the local drug dealers were going wrong. They were selling to people on the streets. Many of their customers were criminals and were in constant contact with the police. This meant to him that their customers had a higher chance of turning the dealers over to the police if they got in trouble. So Ricky decided to sell to regular people who had jobs and homes. He figured that they would be less likely to be in contact with the police, compared to the drug users who were on the streets. Ricky felt that his risk of getting caught and being robbed would be minimized if he followed that plan. He really felt like it was a good plan at the time.

    Ricky's drug of choice to sell was crack and cocaine. It was amazing to him how many working class people had this drug habit. Some of his clients were teachers, construction workers, and he even had some lawyers buy from him. Even though they had those drug habits, they were still able to maintain a job, a home, and a social life. We usually only hear about the crack head zombies walking down the streets giving blow jobs for a hit. Apparently those were not the only crack heads in town. Ricky's plan seemed to be working. He was making a lot of money and he was making it fast. He even bought himself a Lexus. Ricky was a self-proclaimed player, so when he got that car, that really got the women flocking to him. What else could he ask for?

One day while making a delivery of drugs to a customer that lived in an apartment building, a beautiful female caught his eye. Now Ricky was used to delivering to houses, not apartments, but he made an exception because the customer was a good friend of his. When he saw the beautiful woman, he was glad that he made that exception. He began to converse with her and they exchanged phone numbers. Ricky finished his drug delivery and headed home. He ended up calling the woman the same night and they hit it off immediately. They would talk on the phone a couple of times, but he knew that there was not going to be anything serious with her. He just wanted to see if he could have sex with her and how quickly he could do it.

Ricky decided to take the woman out on a date to dinner one night. He figured that if he took her to a nice restaurant, then it would be an easy task to sleep with her. The date went well that night, and afterwards he asked if he could take her to a hotel. She did not really want to go to the hotel that he picked because she was afraid that she would see someone that she knew there. Ricky did not think much of it and dropped her off home. The next night they went out again and he tried to get her to another hotel, but this time she said that she forgot something at home so could he take her to get it. All the way back to her home she kept texting someone on her phone. Ricky thought that it was rude but said nothing to her.

Once at her house, she got out of the car and said she would be right back. Ricky was kind of tired so he let the seat down some to relax. He saw a male walking by the passenger side of his vehicle but thought nothing of it. There was a lot of pedestrian traffic in that area, so it was not unusual to see people walking at odd hours there. It was also was not the safest area to be in after dark I might add.

Ricky was real tired that night so while he was waiting for his date to return, he dozed off a little. All of a sudden, he was awakened by a strange noise. He did not know what it was so he sat up in his seat. He noticed a hole in his windshield. The hole looked like a bullet hole. Ricky then thought to himself that he had been shot. He then looked down and saw blood coming from his stomach. Ricky could see the female he had dropped off jumping up and down yelling something but he could not hear what she was saying. It was as if everything was going in slow motion. Ricky then began to hear someone tapping on the side of his car's window. He looked to his side and saw a male in a ski mask pointing a revolver in the direction of his head. His window was still up but the threat was real. The male told him to get out of the car.

Ricky thought to himself at that moment that he was going to die. He decided to call onto God for help. All of a sudden a voice came into his head and told him to drive off. So he drove off as fast as he could. The masked gunman began shooting at the car, striking Ricky in the arm as he drove away. He was able to drive to nearby friend's house. Ricky got out of the car and stumbled into his friend's gate. As he walked inside his friend's gate, he was met by his friend's father. Ricky told him that he needed help and that he had just been shot. His friend's father told him to get off his property. Ricky begged and pleaded for help, but to no avail. What would you do if you saw your child's friend at your house with gunshot wounds begging for help? I do not think I would kick him off my property; some people just do not want to get involved. Even if it means saving a life, they will not put themselves near the situation. Ricky was able to muster enough energy to call another friend on the phone and told him where he was. After making the phone call Ricky fell to the ground as everything began to look blurry. He can remember calling on God again as he faded out.

    Ricky awoke in the hospital with tubes coming out of his nose. He can remember seeing the friend that he called for help and his friend's girlfriend standing over him. They brought him up to speed on what happened that night and how they got him to the hospital. Ricky had been shot twice, once in the stomach and once in the arm. The doctors were able to get the bullet from out of his stomach but not out of his arm. Ricky would spend a couple of months in the hospital recovering. He had been temporarily paralyzed on his right side. This meant he would have to go through many weeks of physical therapy. Ricky had to learn how to walk all over again. That was a grueling process but he made it through and was able to walk again.

    While in the hospital, Ricky wondered why did God save him. He was nothing but a drug dealer, but God decided to spare his life. The masked gunman could have shot him to death as he drove off. Ricky's tints were not dark in his car. The gunman saw him reaching over, putting the car in drive, and pulling away before he started shooting again. Ricky thought that this had to be God's work. He never held any ill will towards the gunman or the female who may have possibly set him up. Ricky felt that what happened to him was karma. When you are living the criminal life, bad things are bound to happen. Ricky was deep into the criminal life so he felt that it was only a matter of time before something bad was going to happen to him. He did not think that he would almost lose his life, but the game is not a fair one.

When I asked Ricky what got him through this adversity of being shot and nearly killed, he responded that calling on God and forgiving those that harmed him was the key. When he was selling drugs, Ricky was not really practicing his religion like he should have. He had kind of steered away from God. He truly felt that he did not need God at that time in his life. As soon as he was faced with death, God was who he called on in his time of need. When Ricky was released from the hospital he had to figure out his next move. His family told him that when he was in the hospital, he said he was going to preach God's word. Ricky did not remember saying that but he was going to keep his word if he did say it.

Ricky has kept his word and is preaching God's words wherever he goes. We are always debating because my views are not the same as his. A little debate among friends is a good thing. Ricky is no longer selling drugs and has no desire to. He lost his Lexus because he could not keep up with the payments. He now catches the bus and rides his bike where he needs to go. Ricky is not living as lavish as he once was when he sold drugs, but he is alive.

If you are reading this and are going through the

adversity of being shot, you are alive. Cherish every breath that you have. Bask in the sunlight and be thankful for another chance. If you are religious then call upon God for strength and forgive. If you are not religious, then meditate and let go. We are all here on borrowed time. Make your time here meaningful.

YOU CANNOT CHANGE THE PAST, BUT YOU CAN CORRECT THE PRESENT IN ORDER TO CHANGE YOUR FUTURE.

Chapter 10
The Abused

*"We may encounter many defeats
but we must not be defeated."*
~Maya Angelou

I come from a very big family. There are seven of us. I have two brothers and the rest are my sisters. I also have a lot of cousins. I help mentor some of my younger cousins as well as their kids from time to time. One of my favorite female cousins, Samantha, I actually helped raise her growing up. She is about ten years younger than me. I can remember taking her, as well as her siblings, to daycare when they were very young. Samantha was always acting silly as a young child. Being that she was the oldest of her siblings, she took on the role of being a big sister very seriously though. She has grown up to be a very beautiful and responsible adult. Samantha now has a son of her own and is doing the best that she can to raise him. Samantha was not always a responsible adult. Unfortunately, that led her to have dealt with a very big adversity in her life with regards to her son.

It all started after Samantha gave birth to her son James. She was very vulnerable and lonely at the time because James' father did not stick around. Samantha was young and naive at that time. She believed that he would take care of his responsibility even though it did not work out between the two of them. She was wrong and he left her alone to raise James without a father. Samantha decided at that point that she would not date for a while and focus on raising her son. Many times in life, the thing that you vow not to do or partake in, presents itself to see how committed you are to your statement.

For Samantha, it was the guy who lived next door to her by the name of Brian who had been trying to get with her for many years, who presented himself to her. Brian had been trying to get with her for a long time, but Samantha would always turn him down. But after being single for so long after James' father left, she figured she would give Brian a chance. Samantha would go out on a couple of dates with him and feel him out. Brian told her all of the things that she wanted to hear at that time. He told her that he wanted a family and she definitely felt James needed a father figure so she began dating him.

In the beginning of their relationship, everything was good. Isn't it always good in the beginning? Brian would bring her breakfast in bed. He would buy James clothes and shoes to wear without Samantha ever asking him to. He was exhibiting all the qualities in a man that she wanted as well as the qualities of a good father to James. Around that time James was about thirteen months, so naturally he was very clingy to Samantha. Brian would make sure that James was not all up on Samantha. He felt that James needed to be around a man more, so he made it happen. He would always have James by his side. Brian was looking like the man of the year. Remember, monsters wear masks very well. They are masters of deception. If you saw them coming, then they would never be able to have any victims.

Samantha began using drugs around the time she got with Brian, so her judgment was definitely not the best. She was smoking marijuana as her drug of choice. Samantha got up to smoking about four joints a day. She felt that the marijuana calmed her down and made her focus more on any task that she had to complete. Samantha had smoked marijuana before she got with Brian, so she does not blame him for her drug use. Since Brian smoked marijuana as well, her usage gradually increased when she got with him.

As their relationship continued, Samantha would spend more nights sleeping over at Brian's house. Whenever she would spend the night, she would always bring James with her. One night while at Brian's house, James began to cry. This was typical behavior for a one year old child. Brian began to get annoyed with James crying. He began to yell at Samantha and told her that if she did not shut James up that he would kick the both of them out of his house. Samantha was shocked and very upset at what Brian had told her. She never heard Brian speak to her that way, especially concerning her son. Brian apologized for the incident and said that he loved the both of them. In the back of Samantha's mind, she felt that something was very wrong with Brian for making that statement. She did not know how he could threaten to kick her and her one year old son out of his house just because he was crying.

After that incident, things went back to being good for a while. Brian was back to being the standup guy she thought he was. One morning while at Brian's house, Samantha noticed that James was moving kind of weird. He was not walking at that age yet, but he was trying. James appeared to be in pain. Samantha felt that something was wrong with the way that James was moving. She brought it to Brian's attention but he dismissed it and said that nothing was wrong with James. This did not sit right with Samantha, so she took James to the hospital to get examined. While at the hospital, the doctor examined James but no x-rays were done. The doctor told her that it was normal for kids to move in that fashion right before they were about to walk. James was given some pain medication and they were released. Samantha felt better since the doctor told her that and they both went home.

A few weeks after that incident, Samantha began to observe nail marks on James' back and in the palms of his hands. She once again confronted Brian about what she had observed. Brian acknowledged seeing the nail marks, but informed her that he did not know where they came from. Samantha thought that one of the other kids who frequented the house and who were related to Brian was possibly causing the injuries to James. Something in Samantha felt that someone was purposely harming her son and that Brian knew about it because of his nonchalant attitude about the whole situation. Brian was only alone with James for a short amount of time, so she did not suspect him of doing anything to James. Whenever Brian was alone with James, it was usually when Samantha had to go to the store or run a quick errand.

    Samantha had not been working while she was with Brian, so he supported the three of them. In order to help out, Samantha had begun looking for employment. She had finally got an interview after filling out many job applications. Brian was so excited, he really wanted the financial help from Samantha. Samantha had one big problem with regards to making her interview. She did not have anyone to watch James, so she asked Brian if he could do it. Brian did not have a problem watching James. This was the first time that Brian would watch James for a long amount of time. Samantha really wanted this job and did not think anything would happen to James while she was gone. Unfortunately, Samantha did not get the job. She relayed this to Brian over the phone and he was upset. She asked if James was alright and he told her that James was fine.

    As soon as she arrived to the house, Brian said that he had something to tell her. He told her that something was wrong with James. She could hear James screaming in the back of the house. When she saw James, he had a burn mark on the side of his face. Samantha questioned Brian about that and he told her that it was from James' nebulizer. James was also grabbing on to his legs as if something was wrong with them. Samantha felt that something was not right about that situation. She immediately got some ice and put it on his legs. James was in pain all through the night. I know what many of you are thinking, why didn't she go straight to the hospital. This would prove detrimental for her later on. Many times when people are in love, mixed with heavy drug use, they are blinded to the real picture.

Samantha took James to the hospital the next morning. After examining James, the doctor informed her that James had two broken tibias, fractures on his rib cage, a broken shoulder, and a broken femur. They also told her that it looked as if James had been tortured. As I type this, all I can think about is how someone could cause injuries like this to a one year old. This world is truly filled with cowardly monsters. They prey on the weak and those that cannot defend themselves. Brian was six feet four inches tall and weighed two hundred and thirty pounds. James never stood a chance.

Naturally Child Protective Services and the police were called out to the hospital. The investigation was focused on Samantha at first. She was James' mother, so she had to answer to why her son had so many injuries. Samantha told them the same story about her going to a job interview and leaving James with Brian. The doctors informed her and the police that it was impossible for a nebulizer to burn a person's face the way it did James. This meant that Brian had lied about the burn on James' face. Samantha now began to know in her heart that Brian had hurt her son.

Samantha went to confront Brian at his house as to why he had harmed James. He denied doing anything to James. He began to strike Samantha several times in the face with closed fists. He also slammed her on the ground. Samantha was able to get away and call the police. Brian fled the scene before the police arrived. Samantha disregarded her injuries and went back to the hospital to be with her son. James would stay in the hospital for three weeks recovering from his many injuries. He was required to wear a full body cast that went from his chest to his legs for two months after he left the hospital. For an active one year old, it was hard to be stuck in a full body cast. James was at the age of growth and exploration. He was now limited to being confined in a cast around his body

    Physically James recovered from his injuries because he was so young, his bones had not fully developed yet. Mentally, he would suffer for a long time. He had constant nightmares and would awaken frequently throughout the night. Brian was eventually arrested for what he did to James and Samantha, but the State Attorney would not prosecute the case. The state would end up dropping the charges so Brian was eventually released from jail. Samantha was livid at the state's decision not to prosecute. Why was justice not being sought for her son? She would go to the supervisor of the attorney who was handling the case and demanded answers. The supervisor told her that there was not enough evidence which would suggest that Brian hurt James. The jury would question why Samantha waited until the morning to take James to the hospital. They could think that Samantha caused the injuries. The state basically felt that the case was weak. Samantha was told to keep going to school and to continue on with her life.

    This was a very challenging adversity that Samantha had to go through. She was able to get through it by constantly praying and staying close to her family. She was trying to create her own family with Brian, but she had a loving and supportive family all along that she now appreciates. Samantha quit smoking marijuana on the day that she had to take her son to the hospital and has never looked back. She avoids negative people and drama. Samantha surrounds herself around all things positive. She has a new boyfriend who is completely the opposite of Brian. I have met him personally and he is a standup guy, not only by his words, but by his actions as well. James is doing well and is very energetic.

When it comes to our kids, we are the protectors of them until they are able to protect themselves. We need to take that job very seriously. Samantha had many warning signs but she was unable to see clearly until it was too late. If you have or are going through a similar adversity as Samantha, just know that you will make it through it. You cannot change the past, but you can correct the present in order to change your future.

YOUR OUTER WORLD
IS A REFLECTION OF
YOUR INNER WORLD.

Chapter 11

The Lonely One

"If you're lonely when you are alone, you are in bad company."
~Jean-Paul Sartre

The first year of my divorce was an interesting one. It was nothing like what I imagined it would be. I was single and I was ready to mingle. Unfortunately, my shift at work had just changed and I was put on the midnight shift. That made it hard to mingle. If you have never worked the midnight shift, it is one of the loneliest shifts one could work. It is especially lonely if you just got out of a marriage. All I had was time on my hand. I had plenty of time to think about any and everything. I was not going to let my new shift get me down though. I began to search for all those women who flirted with me when I was married. Well, the truth is that they were nowhere to be found. I tried to reach out to some ex-girlfriends, but they were all taken. I even decided to hit the club scene, but it was not the same as it was before I got married. Well it actually was the same, I was not. I was older now. Those women in the club were in their twenties and did not want anything to do with a thirty-two year old. Where was the long line of women waiting for this freshly divorced man? Did I really make the right choice in getting a divorce?

The loneliness really began to set in so I knew I had to do something about it. I decided that I was not going to let that loneliness get the best of me. I was so eager for a date in that first year after my divorce, it did not even make any sense how desperate I was. I like to call that first year of my divorce, my "thirsty for dates" period. I decided that I would try online dating. It seemed like everyone was doing it so why not give it a try. I decided to go with a free online dating site at first. It was a very well known popular site so I figured I would have no problems getting a date there. When it came time to set up my online profile, I was honest in it. I figured women would respect a short, average build, divorced guy with multiple kids. I even put pictures of me sky diving and travelling to different places around the world in there. There was even a picture with me riding a camel on there. Who could resist talking to a guy who rides camels? That would surely get them interested in me.

After a couple of weeks with that profile up, no one made contact with me. I decided that maybe I had to contact them, instead of waiting for the women to contact me. I had to send messages to at least thirty women on that site. I am a writer, so my messages were more than just a simple hello or what's up. I was hitting them with some of my good stuff, but I still got no responses. After being on that site for a couple of months, I only ended up getting one message. The message came from an individual who described themselves as a feminine male. This really could not be my life.

After getting that message from the feminine male, I decided to try a paid dating site. Maybe I would have better luck if I actually invested some money in this thing. The paid site required that a long questionnaire containing about fifty questions be answered before your profile could be set up. There was supposed to be some scientific method being used on the site and it would pair me with the most compatible women. I cannot even lie; the women that the site advised me that were compatible with me were very beautiful. Unfortunately, compatibility has to be a two way street. I never got a response from any of those women either. I began to really question would anyone ever want me. My self-esteem was really damaged from online dating. Let me correct that statement. My self-esteem was damaged prior to online dating, it just did not help it. Many times we blame outside things for what is really an issue going on the inside of us. Your outer world is a reflection of your inner world. I decided to close my online dating profiles and leave those sites alone. If something is not making you feel good, then you need to leave it alone.

My thirst for a date was getting stronger as well as my loneliness. I just wanted somebody to talk to. I did not care where she worked or even if she had a job at all. I began to reflect back on all the women that I have ever dated in my life. I was able to get them back then, so why not now? Maybe my forte was meeting women in person, not online. One night while I was on a break at work getting some tea at an all-night café, I saw this beautiful woman come in. Something in me told me to go and try to get her number, so I listened and made my move. I complimented her on her hair and we engaged in a short conversation. I asked for her number and she gave it to me.

I felt great at that moment. There would be no more lonely nights for me. I believed that I had gotten my grove back at that moment.

I wanted to call her immediately, but I played it cool and waited a few days before I made that call. When I finally spoke to her, our conversation was not that long at first. It did not even matter to me. I just made sure that before I hung up with her that I locked in a confirmation for our first date. I arranged to take her out to a nice place. Our first date would be at a great restaurant located in a well-known casino. On the night of the date, I got to her house around ten and texted her that I was outside. I was so excited. It had been too long since I had been out with a woman. After about twenty minutes, she still had not come out yet. I texted her again and she advised me that she was coming out in a minute. That minute came and went. One hour had past and she still did not come out. Most people would have probably left this woman after waiting that long, but not me. I was desperate and tired of being lonely so I waited. When you are desperate, you are at a disadvantage. You will be susceptible to accepting anything, even if it is not in your best interest. She finally came out after me waiting for almost two hours.

When she came out, she had on a leopard print one piece outfit. I just knew that this was going to be a date to remember. She also had a duffle bag with her when she came to my car. She told me that she brought a change of clothes just in case. I was so confused. Was wardrobe changes a part of first dates now? What did she mean by just in case? I did not question her about it, I was just ready to start the date. When she got into the car, she asked me if I could take her to her cousin's house who stayed up the street. I did not have a problem with that. I waited almost two hours for her to come out, what was one stop going to hurt.

When we got to her cousin's house, her cousin came outside wearing only a bra and some shorts. I could see that she had some clothes in her hand. She proceeded to change clothes right there in the driveway before she got into the car. My date then asked if I could take her cousin to cash her check. First of all, I did not know that people still got physical checks at this day and age. Secondly, it was almost midnight, where was she going to cash this check at? To my surprise there was an all-night check cashing place open. What did I get myself into?

So I took her cousin to cash the check without any problems. After the check was cashed, my date had yet another request for me. She asked me if I could drop her cousin off to a night club that was nearby. Her cousin suspected that her boyfriend was there and she wanted to spy on him. I figured that I had come this far in the date, why not drop her off to the club. The sooner I got rid of her cousin, the sooner me and my date could be alone. The drop off was made, so finally my date and I were on the way to our destination.

During the ride to the casino, my date was on the phone. I thought it was kind of rude, but I just kept the thought to myself. As I was driving, I heard a small thud in the car. I immediately wondered what the sound was. When I looked over into the passenger's seat, I noticed that it was my date's cell phone falling out of her hand. As I took a closer look over at my date, she was knocked out. How could I continue with the date? This woman was actually sleeping in my car. I nudged her and told her that she seemed tired and that we could reschedule the date for another time. She insisted that I just drive slowly to the casino. She told me that all she needed was a few minutes to sleep so she could be rested for the date. Like a dummy, I drove slowly to our destination. I woke her up when we arrived and we went inside. We had to get on an elevator to get to the restaurant. While in the elevator, there were about four people in there. They were all staring fiercely at my date. She did not like that and began to argue with them. I had to pull her away from them quickly once we got to our stop. She was ready to physically fight them all for staring at her. I could not believe what had just happened. I just wanted to get out and eat, not break up a potential fight from an elevator.

While inside the casino, she insisted on holding my hand as we walked. I was very uncomfortable with that. Everyone was staring at us as we walked holding hands. I am most certainly sure it was because of the leopard print one piece outfit that she had on. I was not used to that type of attention. Once we sat down to eat, the conversation was not that bad but I could see that we were in two different worlds.

After eating, we walked around the casino for a while and gambled on a few slot machines. The date had finally come to an end so we got into the car so I could drive her home. I figured that we could talk some more on the way to her house but like clockwork, she fell asleep again. The whole ride to her house, all I could think about was I really that desperate for companionship. Loneliness is a dreadful feeling. We as humans are not meant to be alone; at least that was what I thought at that time.

Once we made it to her house, I woke her up and told her that we had arrived. She looked at me and told me that we could stay in the car and talk for a little while before she went inside. I thought to myself that I was not in a rush. Some more conversation could not hurt. As soon as she made that statement, she rolled over in the seat and went back to sleep. Some of you may be thinking that I am making this up, but I assure you that I could not make up something like this. I could not believe what was happening. Was I in a dream? I sat there for about a minute before I nudged her again to awaken her. She awoke again and said just give her twenty minutes before I wake her again. I am even too embarrassed to type this, but I actually sat there in that car for twenty minutes while she slept. I kept thinking to myself was all she had to do was take a few steps, walk inside her house, and she would be in her bed. Apparently my car must have been very comfortable to her. I had truly hit rock bottom on this date. After the twenty minutes, I woke her up. She gave me a hug and I ensured that she made it in the house safely. She told me to call her as I drove home, but that was not going to happen. I peeled out of that driveway as fast as I could.

I had many other interesting dates with various women during that time period. I tried to date my way out of loneliness, but it did not work. It was not until I focused on myself did that thirst for having to have dates dissipate. An amazing thing began to happen. My loneliness was there no more. I actually began to enjoy my own company. I took myself out and did things that brought me happiness. Everything that I did in my life, it was done with a purpose. As I undertook that journey of self, women began to appear in my life. I was not focused on them, yet they appeared. Life is funny like that sometimes. They were a better quality of women I might add. I was not afraid to go to the movies alone, eat at a restaurant alone, or hit the beach alone. The wonderfully amazing thing was that I was not alone. I was with myself. Because I was so focused on accomplishing my dreams and goals, women wanted to be a part of my life. I had the option of going out with whoever I wanted, whenever I wanted.

If you are going through the adversity of loneliness, it is a tough thing to deal with. Loneliness will have you craving for all types of attention. Many times the people who do not have your best interest at heart will be the ones that you find. If you really think about it, you attract who you are. Even though my date seemed all over the place, I was no better than her. Emotionally I was a mess, and it reflected in the women that I chose to deal with at that time. The thing that you have to realize about loneliness is that you are not really alone. Explore yourself; true happiness is waiting inside of you for you to find it.

IF YOU DO NOT FORGIVE YOURSELF, THEN WHO WILL.

Chapter 12

The Cat Eater

"But we can't go back. We can only go forward"
~Libba Bray

I was born and raised in Miami, Florida. Being from Miami, it meant that I was exposed to a diverse group of people. We have Cubans, Dominicans, Puerto Ricans, Black Americans, and Haitians, to name a few. My family was Haitian. Both of my parents were born and raised in Haiti. My mother migrated here from Haiti via Bahamas with me in her stomach. I was the first born here in the United States. My mother would end up having my little sister here in the U.S. as well a few years later.

Being from a Haitian family our native tongue was Creole. My mother spoke it to us all the time, as well as English. We were fortunate enough to grow up in a bilingual family. Before I started school, we lived in a predominately Haitian neighborhood. Everything seemed so good in those early years growing up in that neighborhood. I could relate with all my friends and Haitian pride flourished in the community. As with many things in life, the good times did not last. We had to move out of that neighborhood and into a new community. This community was full of black Americans. At that young age,

I thought that we were all black Americans, but I was quickly taught otherwise.

I can remember my first lesson in discrimination started around seven years old. I was in this new neighborhood with no friends so I decided to try and see if I could make some. I was a shy kid by nature so it took a while for me to make new friends. I decided to muster up the courage and go play with the kids who were playing outside. As I walked to play with the neighborhood kids, I can remember seeing them picking on another kid who was just sitting there with his head down. I wondered why he had his head down, but I would soon find out why. They kept saying that he was a Haitian and that he ate cats. They taunted him with "cat eater" chants. Tears poured from his face as they kept calling him a Haitian. I thought to myself, why was it wrong to be a Haitian? I never ate a cat before, why were they saying those things. They soon turned their attention to me and asked was I a Haitian. I was so scared and confused at that moment. I had a feeling if I said yes, then my fate could be the same as the kid in tears. I did not want to get beat up or picked on, so I lied. It would be the beginning of an adolescence filled with shame and fear of discrimination.

Elementary school years was a rough time growing up for me. It was as if being Haitian meant you had the plague. The kids would call each other Haitian as a form of an insult. If they found out you were Haitian, they would pick on you and beat you down. My siblings and I would have to run to and from school from those bullies who wanted to jump on us because we were Haitian. In those days Haitian parents would dress their kids up as if they were going to church. We did look sharp I have to admit. Unfortunately we were not going to church, we were going to school. The girls would be forced to wear big fluffy dresses. The boys had to wear collared shirts, slacks with belts, and dress shoes. This was not the look in elementary school, and we paid the price dearly for dressing like that. Playing kickball in dress shoes was rough on my little feet. As I think back on it now, the way we dressed was the same way that black Americans dressed during the fifties and sixties. Now they were picking on us for dressing how they used to dress, life is funny that way sometimes.

In school I would deny being a Haitian anytime I was asked. I was asked it a lot because I was told that I looked like a Haitian, if one could look like a Haitian. The biggest giveaway for me though was my first name, Pijhon. I hated my first name. The kids would always make fun of it. I would always think why my parents gave me that name. They could have just named me John. That was a simple name with no confusion.

One day I decided that no one would not call me Pijhon anymore, my new name would be Pj. Every time someone would say my name, I would answer Pj what. I know it sounds crazy, and at first it was crazy saying Pj what every time I was called. After a while, everyone began calling me Pj. I just really did not like people judging me before they even knew me. When I looked in the mirror, I did not like what I saw. Since I had carried shame on the inside at that time, of course I would not like the reflection on the outside.

It was as if I was living a double life. I did not talk to my mother or siblings about what was going on; I just kept it to myself. Besides being ashamed of my culture, I was ashamed of my home. My family was very poor and at one point we lived in an apartment on top of a store. That place was very bad, but it was the best that my mother could find at the time. We had rats all over that place. When I say rats, I mean mini puppy rats. Those rats were not scared of us at all. If we spotted them, we would stomp our feet and they would not even move. They were so brazen that they would steal food out of the pots on the stove while the food was still being cooked. We even tried to put cats in the house to kill them, but those gladiator rats ran them off. I did not want to invite any of my friends over because of the fear that they would find out that I was Haitian and of the shame that I had over where I lived. That was a lot of pressure for a kid.

Since I did not want my friends to come over to my house, I would always go to theirs. We would play games and I would pray that they would want me to stay for dinner because I was always hungry. Food was scarce at my house because it was seven of us and it was tough for my mom being a single parent. When my friends would ask if I wanted to stay for dinner, I always said yes. They could have been serving me poison; it would have been still a yes from me.

After a while, my frieds began to question me on where I lived. I always gave them a general area but never would I give them the exact location. I felt as if they would not want to be my friend anymore if they knew the truth.

Many times after spending time at their house, their parents would offer me rides home because it was late. I declined the first few times, but after a while their parents insisted on taking me home. When their parents would drop me home, I would have them drop me a block away. Once I was out of the car, I would walk to a random gate and wave them off. As soon as they left, I would walk the rest of the way home. That worked for a while, but my friends soon began comparing notes on where their parents dropped me off at. The mistake I made was walking to different gates, instead of the same ones, so they became suspicious.

One day as I was walking home from school, I entered the apartment building just like I normally did. This time was different though. As I looked behind me, I saw three of my friends coming to the building. They had followed me home from school. I would have never expected that they would go to those lengths to discover where I lived. My heart dropped. I quickly ran inside and hid in a storage room. I began praying that they did not see me. They began yelling my name all throughout the building. My heart was racing. I was about to be exposed. They were going from door to door asking the tenants did I live there. All I kept thinking was how did I not see them behind me. It takes so much energy to keep a lie going. Luckily for me one of the neighbors ran them off. My secret was still safe.

My shame of being a Haitian was so deep that I did not even speak the language anymore. I understood it but purposely did not speak it. I figured that if I did not use it, then I would forget it. I would answer my mother in

English if she spoke to me in Creole. I did not want any part of being a Haitian. I was so committed to that lie. When you are not standing in your truth, things never seem right. The mask of shame was worn faithfully by me for a long time.

    Whenever the topic of talking about Haitians came up in school, I would stay quiet. I just prayed that they did not question me. Sometimes the conversations would be dirty Haitians this, or cat eaters that. My people's name was being dragged through the mud as I cowered in silence. I can remember one time while being in the fourth grade we had a new student come into our class. She did not speak any English, only Creole. Naturally my teacher called upon me to talk to her. My teacher announced in front of the class that I knew two languages, English and Creole. Why, why, why did she do that to me? The whole class looked at me like I had just been shot. My fourth grade life was over. I just went over to the new girl and spoke to her in English. She just looked at me as if I was crazy and I went back to my seat to die.

    Every year in elementary it was the same thing for me, I was protecting that lie as best as I could. When I started liking girls, it was usually a deal breaker if they found out that I was Haitian. They would call me cute but it stopped at that. The unfortunate actions of my shame robbed me of staying fluent in my native language and culture. I was told that my people were dirty and ate cats. I was not taught to have pride for my culture. The rest of my siblings spoke Creole very well as I chose not to speak it at all.

As I got older, the attitude was changing on being a Haitian. The younger generation had more pride than my generation. Instead of being bullied, the younger generation was fighting back. Haitian gangs emerged and they were some of the most ruthless individuals you could ever meet. Zoe Pound was one of the most highly publicized Haitian gangs in the city. They were heavy in the drug trade as well as responsible for many violent killings. This put Haitians on the map as a dangerous group of people who did not play around. The same women that were turning their noses up at us, now wanted to date us. Every girl wanted a Haitian man. The guys that used to bully us, now wanted to be friends with us. It is amazing how things changed. There was even a famous song, *I'm a Zoe,* by Black Dada that had all the Haitians coming out to represent for Haiti, even the closet Haitians like myself. It felt good to hear that song being played on the mainstream radio stations.

There was also Haitian Flag Day. This is the day in which Haiti's flag is celebrated. It is a celebration of Haiti's independence from French rule. Growing up, I never saw it really represented in my city. As I got older, it became more and more popular. Everyone was wearing Haiti's colors on that day waving their flags high and proud.

The results of my shame were plentiful. I can barely speak Creole now. I understand it well but speaking it clearly is another thing. I have been in many situations where I have had to translate for Haitian people who spoke no English and it was not an easy task. My Creole is so bad at times that the English speakers around me say that my Creole sucks, and they do not even speak the language. My kids do not know the language because I could not teach it to them. The language will die with me and that is unfortunate for them. I have robbed them of knowing such a beautiful language.

The adversity of shame is a very tough thing to get over. Unlike many other adversities, shame is internal. It will eat away at you until it is either addressed or it has consumed all of you. I was put in many situations where I had to face my shame, which led me to overcome it. The friends that I thought would not want to be my friend because of me being a Haitian, could care less about it. They loved my personality and cherished my friendship.

The key thing to overcoming shame is forgiveness. You have to forgive yourself for the shame that you have carried. I am now able to embrace my culture as well as work on speaking the language better. If shame is your adversity, forgive yourself for carrying it. If you do not forgive yourself, then who will.

YOU HAVE THE ULTIMATE CONTROL OVER YOUR LIFE.

Chapter 13

The End

"Expect problems and eat them for breakfast"
~Alfred A. Montapert

This thing called life is a hell of a ride to be on. We have our highs, as well as our lows. Some of those lows involve some sort of adversity. In this book there have been many adversities discussed. With regards to the adversity of divorce, it is a very traumatic thing to deal with. It is like dealing with the death of person, instead it is the death of a family. But it does not have to be. No one says that divorce has to be ugly. You can choose not to be vindictive. Your spouse may be, but you cannot control that. You can only control your own thoughts and actions. I made a conscious effort to think about the best thing for my kids throughout the entire process. When I did this, positive results came.

Your life is not over just because your marriage is. Just remember what my professor told me, you can hit that reset button on your life as many times as you want. If a marriage is not right or healthy for you, get out of it. If you have tried everything in your power to make it work, then be at peace with the notion that you did your best. I know that it is a scary thing to go through, but just know that good actions and intentions are rewarded. Time is a precious thing that we have. Would you rather enjoy that time in growth and happiness, or in despair and anger? Divorce is rough, but it can be overcome. I did it and if you are going through it, you will overcome it as well.

The adversity of sexual molestation is an issue that plagues many people. The perpetrators of many of these acts are family members or close family friends. In this book, three women's experiences were shared. Patricia was molested by her mother's boyfriend at five years old. Heather was molested by her cousin at ten years old, and Gina was eight when she was molested by her step-father. These women had to go through their adversity at an early age. It set the narrative on how many of their lives would turn out. Heather was able to overcome her situation by being strong and using it as motivation to persevere through life. Gina was able to get an apology and to forgive her molester. Patricia is still struggling with overcoming her adversity but she is still in the fight.

Everyone who is dealing with sexual molestation has their own way of dealing with it. Talking about what happened is the first step on the path to healing. I encourage parents of young children to be cautious and observant of whom you bring into your kids' lives. The wrong choice could have a lifelong effect on you and your kids. We were created with intuition for a reason. If it does not feel right, investigate it and do something about it. We need to protect the young until they are old enough to protect themselves.

The adversity of heartbreak is something that can truly impact one's life. When we fall in love, it is such a beautiful thing. There is just something inherently natural about being in love. I think that deep down inside we all strive to find the right one to experience it with. Unfortunately, when the love is ripped from us, heartbreak appears. My first heartbreak was fortunate enough to happen early in my life. She was my first everything and she wanted nothing to do with me anymore. I was sick to my stomach.

The experience of that heartbreak caused me to grow up real quick and overcome it. I was able to overcome the adversity of heartbreak through getting out of the house and hanging with friends. I also talked to other women which helped a whole lot. Ultimately, the cure of the heartbreak was time. There is no set time on how long it will take for your heart to heal. Just know that before long the pain will be gone and you will be free to love again.

Being incarcerated is an adversity that many inflict upon themselves. With regards to Richard, he was living a life filled with crime. He came from a home that had a working mother and father that taught him right from wrong. Those teachings fell on deaf ears because Richard became a criminal who broke into people's homes and robbed drug dealers. It was not until he was sent to prison on a seventeen year sentence did he truly discover why he was behaving the way that he was. Richard's self-inflicted adversity of being incarcerated was caused by him being bullied as a child and not being accepted by his peers. It took for him to be a part of a program that focused on self-reflection for him to realize what was causing his behavior. The years and years of him putting up walls to hide his pain were torn down and his pain was healed. Everyone who is incarcerated may not suffer from the same issues as Richard, but self-reflection is the key into understanding one's behavior. If you are going to be incarcerated, why not use that time to improve upon yourself.

When it comes to spiritual adversity, religion plays a big role in it. I struggled with religion for a very long time. Even though I was raised as a Christian, I veered away from many religious values and beliefs that were taught to me. I thought that religion was the key to salvation, but when I found flaws in it my faith in it dissipated. I did not want anything to do with it. It was not until I discovered the statement of God is love and love is God did everything truly make sense to me. That statement put things into perspective for me.

It did not matter what religion a person practiced, as long as love was being taught, it was alright with me. Many of us do not have a say in what religious sect that we will be raised in. Whatever our parents are practicing will be what they teach us. Once we are old enough, we can choose to worship whatever we want. The adversity of a spiritual kind is a very tough thing to get through. I believe that many questions that you have can be answered from within and from guidance from a trusted friend. I challenge you to ask questions. You were made an intelligent being for a reason, use it.

I passed one of the toughest boot camps in the military, The United States Marine Corps boot camp. There were many adversities in my way to accomplishing the goal of becoming a Marine. One of the most difficult was passing the swimming qualifications. I had no experience with swimming and only had a week to pass or face being sent back in training, which meant it would take longer for me to graduate. Lack of confidence in my ability to pass and the fear of drowning were my two main obstacles.

It was not until I was left in the water to drown, did my fear of drowning disappear. My worst fear had come true and I survived. There was no more fear after that. Without that fear, my confidence came through and I passed the swim qualification and ultimately became a United States Marine. If fear is your adversity, there is only one way to go. That direction is straight through it. It will be scary but well worth it in the end.

Being shot has to be one of the most terrifying and traumatic adversities that a person can go through. Ricky was a local drug dealer who had the unfortunate experience of being shot twice in the body. He nearly lost his life living a life of crime that he knew was not right. He credits God for saving his life and forgiving those that harmed him.

Without forgiveness or calling on God, Ricky felt that he would have never made it out that hospital alive. Although Ricky was a drug dealer and his lifestyle may have caused him to get shot, many people get shot that are not engaged in criminal activities. Either way, calling upon your faith and even forgiving those that hurt you can help you heal from the adversity of being shot. I know that is easier said than done, but I challenge you to try it. If it does not work, you can always go back to holding on to the hate of them.

Samantha had to overcome the adversity of her son being physically abused by her boyfriend. Due to her heavy drug use while she was with her boyfriend, this caused her to not make the best decisions which could have protected her son from being abused. Her boyfriend was arrested for the crime but the case was dropped due to questions on why she did not immediately take her son to get treatment.

Her son would ultimately recover from the injuries but Samantha has to carry that burden with her for the rest of her life. Samantha dealt with that adversity by surrounding herself with positive people and dating a guy who brings the best out of her. Mistakes cannot be taken away and dwelling on them does you no good. All you can do is learn from them and be the best possible person that you can be.

The adversity of loneliness was something that I never imagined after my divorce. I became thirsty for dates, but the real thirst was for companionship. I had no luck finding anyone using online dating services. I had to find dates the old fashion way, in person. Even then, my desperation caused me to put myself in situations that were not the best for me.

It was not until I focused on me, did things start to change. I was no longer looking for dates, women came looking for me. I was comfortable being alone and focusing on the goals that I had set for myself. When I did that, happiness came to me. The fact was that I was never alone; I just did not see it. I had to look deep within and realize that the joy that I was looking for from other people was inside of me the whole time.

The adversity of shame is one that I carried with me growing up. I was ashamed of being a Haitian and being poor. That shame caused me to miss out on speaking my family's native tongue proficiently and being unable to pass the language on to my kids. Shame is a heavy burden to carry; it weighs in your heart and your soul. Ultimately, whatever you are hiding from will present itself to you one day and you will have to face it.

If you are dealing with shame, the way to heal it is through forgiveness. I forgave myself for carrying it and embraced my culture. Whatever shame you are carrying, just let it go. Forgive yourself for having it and move on. A burden will be lifted and you will be able to live your life the way that it is truly meant to be.

About the Author

Pijhon "PJ" Valcourt is a Certified Life Coach who focuses on issues of health, wealth, and relationships. He helps his clients discover their life's true purpose and coaches them in accomplishing their goals.

He is also a Professional Inspirational Speaker who has been presenting to the youth in schools around his city for over 13 years on various topics such as anti-bullying, conflict resolution, and empowerment. He is the CEO of Life Purpose Living Inc., a company which focuses on helping individuals transform their lives.

Pijhon is a proud father who enjoys spending time with his children. He currently resides in Miami, Florida.
www.lifecoachpj.com

www.ingramcontent.com/pod-product-compliance
Lightning Source LLC
LaVergne TN
LVHW011948070526
838202LV00054B/4847